KIDS STUFF

ITALIAN

KIDS STUFF ---- ITALIAN

Easy Italian Phrases to Teach Your Kids

Therese Slevin Pirz

BILINGUAL KIDS SERIES

CHOU CHOU PRESS
4 Whimbrel Court
Okatie, SC 29909
www.Bilingualkids.com

Printed in the United States of America.

First Edition.
Library of Congress Catalog No. 97-77713

ISBN 0-9606140-8-7

Order direct from the publisher:

Chou Chou Press
4 Whimbrel Court
Okatie, SC 29909
www.Bilingualkids.com

CONTENTS

PART 3   VOCABULARY - Hundreds of additional words you can insert in a variety of sentences throughout the book that are situation-appropriate.

Note: To avoid the constant use of "he or she," and in the interest of clarity, the author has elected to use masculine pronouns in those chapters which contain paragraph information.

Child's name:_____

Received this book from:_____

Occasion:_____Date:_____

First indication of child's understanding Italian:_____

_____

Child's first Italian word:_____

Child's favorite Italian word:_____

Favorite Italian books or stories:_____

_____

_____

Favorite Italian songs:_____

_____

Favorite things to do in Italian:_____

_____

_____

ACKNOWLEDGEMENTS

I wish to thank two fine gentlemen for their efforts on behalf of this project. Without them this book would have remained a dream . Anton Pirz, a special grandfather; Stephano Morel, an outstanding colleague.

In addition, special acknowledgement is extended to Tara Kelly and Michele Lella who gave the original manuscript their timely touch.

PREFACE

It has been several years since <u>Speak Spanish to Your Baby</u> and <u>Speak French to Your Baby</u> have been published. I have received many requests for an Italian edition. It took until now to finally finish due, in most part, to the demands of raising two children and pursuing another career.

I hope that this book will provide encouragement and practical assistance for those of you who wish to have your children fluent in a second language or just simply want to expose them to the language of another culture-- rich in the arts, music, architecture, cuisine and many other influences.

For those of you who start early or those who arrive at foreign language learning for your older children this book, with its over 1,000 sentences, is an invaluable resource.

Good luck with this adventure. Make it <u>FUN</u>! (The longest chapter is "Playing" !)

To my husband
for his strength and fortitude

To Joseph
for sharing foreign
languages with me

To Raymond
for making me
grow

PART 1

Little Kids

SECOND AND THIRD MONTHS

During these months your baby's listening sense is developing to the point where he is looking for sound sources. He is able to distinguish speech from other sounds. All of his waking hours are spent watching, listening and absorbing the sights and sounds around him.

Che cos'è quello?
Keh koh-ZEH KWEHL-loh?
What is that?

È un cavallo.
Eh oon kah-VAH-loh.
It's a horse.

Che cosa senti?
Keh KOH-zah SEHN-tee?
What do you hear?

Che chiasso!
Keh kee-AHS-soh!
What a noise!

Ti ho fatto paura?
Tee oh FAHT-toh pah-OO-rah?
Did I frighten you?

Che cosa stai dicendo?
Keh KOH-zah stai dee-CHEHN-doh?
What are you saying?

Canti molto bene.
KAHN-tee MOHL-toh BEH-neh.
How beautifully you sing.

Sei un chiacchierone!
Say oon kyahk-kyeh-ROHN-eh!
How talkative you are!

Vieni qua. Siediti.
Vee-EH-nee kwah. SYEH-dee-tee.
Come on . Sit up.

Siediti sulle mie ginocchia.
SYEH-dee-tee SUHL-leh MEE-yeh jee-NOHK-kyah.
Sit on my lap.

Alza la testa.
AHL-tzah lah TEH-stah.
Raise your head.

Prendi!
PREHN-dee!
Take it!

Tieni il sonaglio.
Tee-YEH-nee eel soh-NAH-lyoh.
Hold the rattle.

Molla!
MOHL-lah!
Let go!

A che cosa stai guardando?
Ah keh KOH-zah stai gwahr-DAHN-doh?
What are you looking at?

A cosa stai pensando?
Ah KOH-zah stai pehn-SAHN-doh?
What are you thinking about?

Fammi vedere come muovi le tue braccia!
FAHM-mee veh-DEH-reh KOH-meh MWOH-vee leh TOO-eh BRAH-chee-ah!
Let me see how you move your arms!

Chi sono io?
Kee SOH-noh EE-oh?
Who am I ?

Chi è?
Kee eh?
Who is it?

È/ tuo fratello/ tua sorella.
Eh/ TOO-oh frah-TEHL-loh/ TOO-ah soh-REHL-lah.
It's / your brother / your sister.

Ti piacciono le banane?
Tee pee-YAH-choh-noh leh bah-NAH-neh?
Do you like bananas?

È/ grande/ piccolo.
Eh/ GRAHN-deh/ PEEK-koh-loh.
It's / large/ small.

È piccolo/ piccola.
Eh PEEK-koh-loh/ PEEK-koh-lah.
It's small. (m/f)

È alto.
Eh AHL-toh.
He is tall.

È alta.
Eh AHL-tah.
She is tall.

Ecco il tuo naso, orecchio.
EHK-koh eel TOO-oh NAH-zoh, oh-REHK-kyoh.
Here is your nose, ear.

Ecco la tua bocca.
EHK-koh lah TOO-ah BOHK-kah.
Here is your mouth.

Sorridi! Mostrami un bel sorriso!
Sohr-REE-dee! MOHS-trah-mee oon behl sohr-REE-soh!
Smile! Show me a nice smile!

Che storia lunga!
Keh STOH-ree-ah LOON-gah!
What a long story!

FOURTH, FIFTH AND SIXTH MONTHS

Your baby now proceeds to make new sounds for himself and imitates tones of anger, comfort, or praise. This involves intent listening on his part. He particularly enjoys rhythmic verses such as nursery rhymes. Learn several rhymes. Tell him the names of those items that he spends so much time seeing and observing every day.

Dove vai?
DOH-veh vai?
Where are you going?

Piano!
Pee-YAH-noh!
Slowly!

Alzati.
AHL-tzah-tee.
Get up.

Stai in piedi.
Stai een PYEH-dee.
Stand up.

Guarda...
GWAHR-dah...
Look at...

Vedi...?
VEH-dee...?
Do you see...?

Girati.
Jeeh-RAH-tee.
Turn around.

Puoi tenere il topo?
Pwoy teh-NEH-reh eel TOH-poh?
Can you hold the mouse?

Che cosa hai in bocca?
Keh KOH-zah ai een BOHK-kah?
What do you have in your mouth?

Non puoi mettere quello in bocca.
Nohn pwoy MEHT-teh-reh KWEHL-loh een BOHK-kah.
You cannot put that in your mouth.

Non dare calci!
Nohn DAH-reh KAHL-chee!
No kicking!

Non schizzare!
Nohn SKEET-zah-reh!
No splashing!

Non darmi dei calci!
Nohn DAHR-mee DEH-ee KAHL-chee!
Don't kick me!

Come tiri calci!
KOH-meh TEE-ree KAHL-chee!
How you kick!

Mi stai bagnando!
Mee stai bah-NYAHN-doh!
You are getting me wet!

Ecco un po' di banana.
EHK-koh oon poh dee bah-NAH-nah.
Here is some banana.

Mangia il pane.
MAHN-jyah eel PAH-neh.
Eat the bread.

Non piangere.
Nohn pee-AHN-jeh-reh.
Don't cry.

Perchè stai piangendo?
Pehr-KEH stai pee-ahn-JEHN-doh?
Why are you crying?

Chi è nello specchio?
Kee eh NEHL-loh SPEHK-kyoh?
Who is that in the mirror?

Dov'è il sonaglio?
DOH-veh eel soh-NAH-lyoh?
Where is the rattle?

Dove sono le costruzioni?
DOH-veh SOH-noh leh koh-stroo-TZYOHN-ee?
Where are the blocks?

Vuoi giocare con la palla?
Vwoy jyoh-KAH-reh kohn lah PAHL-lah?
Do you want to play with the ball?

SEVENTH, EIGHTH AND NINTH MONTHS

Your baby's attention and concentration are increasing. Continue to converse with him in the second language describing objects and activities. He understands what you say, and can follow instructions (if he wants to) such as, "Come here," "Clap your hands."

Picture books and magazines will hold his attention at this time. Use them to expand his knowledge of every-day living.

During these months you've found new friends having a common bond -- children. Perhaps it's time to look at "networking" with other Moms to see if others would like to join you and your youngster in learning Italian. You could advertise in your local newspaper, bulletin board or library. Perhaps your library could help out by being the place to meet with your group.

Vieni dalla mammina.
Vee-EH-nee DAHL-lah mahm-MEE-nah.
Come to mommy.

Guarda come vai!
GWAHR-dah KOH-meh vai!
Look how you go!

Siedi diritto.
SYEH-dee dee-REET-toh.
Sit up straight.

Guarda che bei denti!
GWAHR-dah keh bay DEHN-tee!
Look at those teeth!

Ti fanno male i denti?
Tee FAHN-noh MAH-leh ee DEHN-tee?
Do your teeth hurt?

Fammi vedere come cammini.
FAHM-mee veh-DEH-reh KOH-meh kahm-MEE-nee.
Let's see how you walk.

Non così forte!
Nohn koh-ZEE FOHR-teh!
Not so loud!

Suona il tamburo!
SWOH-nah eel tahm-BOO-roh!
Bang the drum!

Suona il campanello!
SWOH-nah eel kahm-pah-NEHL-loh!
Ring the bell!

Che musica!
Keh MOO-zee-kah!
What music!

Suona un'altra canzone.
SWOH-nah oon AHL-trah kahn-TSOHN-eh.
Play another song.

Ecco una tazza.
EHK-koh OO-nah TAHTS-tsah.
Here is a cup.

Batti le mani.
BAHT-tee leh MAH-nee.
Clap your hands.

Ecco un bambino come te.
EHK-koh oon bahm-BEE-noh KOH-meh teh.
Here is a baby like you.

Dove sono i piedi del bambino? (m)
DOV-veh SOH-noh ee pee-EH-dee dehl bahm-BEE-noh?
Where are the feet of the baby?

Dove sono gli occhi della bambina? (f)
DOH-veh SOH-noh lee OHK-kee DEHL-lah bahm-BEE-nah?
Where are the eyes of the baby?

Non aver paura. Va bene.
Nohn ah-VEHR pah-OOR-ah. Vah BEH-neh.
Don't be afraid. It's okay.

La mamma sta qui.
Lah MAHM-mah stah kwee.
Mommy is here.

Vengo! Vengo a prenderti!
VEHN-goh! VEHN-goh ah prehn-DEHR-tee!
I'm coming! I'm coming to get you!

Preso!
PREH-zoh!
Got-cha!

Di ' "Arrivederci."
Dee, Ahr-ree-veh-DEHR-chee.
Say, "Good-bye."

Fai ciao con la manina.
Fai chyow kohn lah mah-NEE-nah.
Wave good-bye.

Non ti piace...?
Nohn tee pee-AH-cheh...?
Don't you like...?

Non vuoi...?
Nohn vwoy...?
Don't you want...?

TENTH, ELEVENTH AND TWELFTH MONTHS

Your baby continues to exhibit understanding of everyday vocabulary which you use in the second language. As evidence of this, ask him to show you different objects. He cannot, as yet, pronounce their names, but he can point to them when asked. His vocabulary can be extended to include descriptions of what others are doing around him and the "tools" that he uses in imitation of these activities. (A list of tools and appliances is included in this guide.)

Expand your baby's world by taking him shopping and naming those items that become familiar to him during these trips.

Sta in piedi da solo il bambino.
    Stah een pee-EH-dee dah SOH-loh eel bahm-BEE-noh.
        Baby is standing all by himself.

Sta in piedi da sola la bambina.
    Stah een pee-EH-dee dah SOH-lah lah bahm-BEE-nah.
        Baby is standing all by herself.

Hai fatto il tuo primo passo!
    Ai FAHT-toh eel TOO-oh PREE-moh PAHS-soh!
        You have taken your first step!

                        Camminiamo un po'.
                Kahm-mee-NYAH-moh oon poh.
                        Let's take a little walk.

Prendi la mia mano.
PREHN-dee lah MEE-ah MAH-noh.
Take my hand.

Siediti sulla tua sedia.
SYEH-dee-tee SUHL-lah TOO-ah SEH-dee-ah.
Sit on your chair.

Attento/ attenta/ allo scalino.
Aht-TEHN-toh/ aht-TEHN-tah/ AHL-loh skah-LEE-noh.
Watch (m/f) the step.

Sali le scale (fino alla fine).
SAH-lee leh SKAH-leh (FEE-noh AHL-lah FEE-neh).
Climb the stairs (right to the top).

Non girarti a metà.
Nohn jee-RAHR-tee ah meh-TAH.
Don't turn around half-way.

Fai attenzione quando scendi le scale.
Fai aht-tehn-ZYOH-neh KWAHN-doh SHEHN-dee leh SKAH-leh.
Come down the stairs carefully.

Metti il peide nei pantaloni.
MEHT-tee eel pee-EH-deh nay pahn-tah-LOH-nee.
Put your foot into the pants.

Tira il braccio fuori dalla manica.
TEE-rah eel BRACH-choh FWOH-ree DAHL-lah mah-NEE-kah.
Pull your arm out of the sleeve.

Papà ti metterà il pigiama.
Pah-PAH tee meht-teh-RAH eel pee-jee-AH-mah.
Daddy will put on your pajamas.

Vai a prendere le tue scarpe nouve.
Vai ah PREHN-deh-reh leh TOO-eh SKAHR-peh NWOH-veh.
Go get your new shoes.

Mangia la carne.
MAHN-jyah lah KAHR-neh.
Eat the meat.

Come mangi bene!
KOH-meh MAHN-jee BEH-neh!
How well you eat!

Ne vuoi ancora?
Neh vwoy ahn-KOH-rah?
Would you like more?

Che cosa hai in mano?
Keh KOH-zah ai een MAH-noh?
What do you have in your hand?

Metti le molliche nel piatto.
MEHT-tee leh mohl-LEE-keh nehl pee-AHT-toh.
Put the crumbs on the plate.

Dammelo/ Dammela.
DAH-meh-loh/ DAH-meh-lah.
Give it (m/f) to me.

Lascialo/ Lasciala. (m/f)
LAH-shyah-loh/ LAH-shyah-lah.
Let go of it . (m/f)

Non toccare.
Nohn tohk-KAH-reh.
Don't touch.

Prendi il mattoncino.
PREHN-dee eel maht-tohn-CHEE-noh.
Get the block.

Vai a prendere la palla.
Vai ah PREHN-deh-reh lah PAHL-lah.
Go get the ball.

Non romperlo/ romperla. (m/f)
Nohn ROHM-pehr-loh/ ROHM-pehr-lah.
Don't break it. (m/f)

Stai attento/ a (m/f) all'orsacchiotto.
Stai aht-TEHN-toh/ tah ahl-lohr-sahk-KYOHT-toh.
Take good care of Teddy.

Dai da mangiare alla tua bambola.
Dai dah mahn-JYAH-reh AHL-lah TOO-ah BAHM-boh-lah.
Feed your doll.

Dagli/ Dalle un tè.
DAH-lyee/ DAHL-leh oon teh.
Give him/ her some tea.

Non è piacevole l'acqua?
Nohn eh pee-yah-CHEH-voh-leh LAH-kwah?
Doesn't the water feel nice?

Non mangiare il sapone.
Nohn mahn-JYAH-reh eel sah-POH-neh.
Don't eat the soap.

Non puoi stare in piedi nella vasca.
Nohn pwoy STAH-reh een pee-EH-dee NEHL-lah VAHS-kah.
You cannot stand in the tub.

Laviamo la schiena.
Lah-vee-AH-moh lah skee-EH-nah.
Let's wash your back.

Accarezza il cane dolcemente.
Ahk-kah-REHTZ-tzah eel KAH-neh dohl-cheh-MEHN-teh.
Pet the dog gently.

Stai sul sedile.
Stai suhl seh-DEE-leh.
Stay in the seat.

Dov'è la giraffa in questa pagina?
DOH-veh lah jee-RAHF-fah een KWEH-stah PAH-jee-nah?
Where is the giraffe on this page?

Il bambino è contento.
Eel bam-BEE-noh eh kohn-TEHN-toh.
Baby (m) is happy.

La bambina è contenta.
Lah bam-BEE-nah eh kohn-TEHN-tah.
Baby (f) is happy.

Il bambino/ la bambina è triste.
Eel bam-BEE-noh/ lah bam-BEE-nah eh TREE-steh.
Baby (m/f) is sad.

Non essere arrabbiato/a.
Nohn EHS-seh-reh ahr-rahb-bee-AH-toh/ tah.
Don't be angry.

Non arrabbiarti con me.
Nohn ahr-rahb-bee-AHR-tee kohn meh.
Don't get angry with me.

È tempo di fare un pisolino.
Eh TEHM-poh dee FAH-reh oon pee-soh-LEE-noh.
It's time for a nap.

Hai fatto un buon pisolino.
Ai FAHT-toh oon bwohn pee-soh-LEE-noh.
You had a good nap.

PART 2

Not-So-Little Kids

INSTRUCTIONS AND PROPOSALS

Here are listed all kinds of directions, suggestions, proposals and even commands for your child. And when all the urging and cautions are administered and you don't get the right response, there's always "...perchè lo dico io!" (...because I say so!") -- appropriate justification in any language.

Non dare più calci/ pugni.
Nohn DAH-reh pyoo KAHL-chee/
POO-nyee.

Stop kicking/ hitting.

Basta mordere/ piangere.
BAH-stah mohr-DEH-reh/
PYAHN-jeh-reh.

Stop biting/ crying.

Non mordere.
Nohn MOHR-deh-reh.

No biting.

Non piangere.
Nohn PYAHN-jeh-reh.

No crying.

Non mangiare.
Nohn mahn-JYAH-reh.

No eating.

Instructions and Proposals

Fermati! Fehr-MAH-tee!	Stop!
Mi fa male. Mee fah MAH-leh.	That hurts me.
Non entrare! Nohn ehn-TRAH-reh!	Don't go in!
Dammi la mano. DAH-mee lah MAH-noh.	Give me your hand.
Non darmi... Nohn DAHR-mee...	Don't give me...
Non fare tanto chiasso. Nohn FAH-reh TAHN-toh kee-AHS-soh.	Don't make so much noise.
Silenzio, per piacere. See-LEHN-tsee-oh,pehr pee-ah-CHEH-reh.	Quiet, please.
Stai zitto/a. (m/f) Stai DZEE-toh/ tah..	Be quiet.
Non domandarmelo di nuovo. Nohn doh-mahn-DAHR-meh-loh dee NWOH-voh.	Don't ask me again.
Sono occupato/a. (m/f) SOH-noh ohk-koo-PAH-toh/tah.	I'm busy.
Ho fretta. Oh FREHT-tah.	I'm in a hurry.
Devo andare. DEH-voh ahn-DAH-reh.	I must go.
Ritornerò più tardi. Ree-tohr-neh-ROH pyoo TAHR-dee.	I'll come back later.

Aspetta! (un momento)
Ahs-PEHT-tah! (oon moh-MEHN-toh)

Wait! (a moment)

Rimani là.
Ree-MAHN-nee lah.

Stay there.

Vengo subito momento.
VEHN-goh soo-BEE-toh moh-MEHN-toh.

I'm coming in a moment.

Non muoverti.
Nohn MWOH-ver-tee.

Don't move.

Aspetta fino che ritorno.
Ahs-PEHT-tah FEE-noh keh ree-
TOHR-noh.

Wait until I come back.

Non andar via.
Nohn ahn-DAHR VEE-ah.

Don't go away.

Non lo fare più.
Nohn loh FAH-reh pyoo.

Stop doing that.

Vieni via di là.
Vee-EH-nee VEE-ah dee lah.

Come away from there.

Fai quel che ti dico!
Fai kwehl keh tee DEE-koh!

Do what I tell you!

Fai quello che vuoi.
Fai KWEHL-loh keh vwoy.

Do what you like.

Non darmi problemi.
Nohn DAHR-mee proh-BLEHM-ee.

Don't give me trouble.

Non disubbidirmi.
Nohn deez-oob-bee-DEER-mee.

Don't disobey me.

Non fate a pugni.
Nohn FAH-teh ah POO-nyee.

Don't fight.

Fate a turno.
FAH-teh ah TOOR-noh.

Take turns.

Non bisticciate!
Nohn bees-tee-chee-AH-teh!

Don't quarrel with one another.

Lascialo stare.
LAH-shyah-loh STAH-reh.

Leave him alone.
Leave that alone.

Lascia stare il gatto.
LAH-shyah STAH-reh eel GAHT-toh.

Leave the cat alone.

Non stuzzicarlo.
Nohn stootz-tzee-KAHR-loh.

Don't tease him.

Non toccare. È sporco.
Nohn tohk-KAH-reh. Eh SPOHR-koh.

Don't touch that. It's dirty.

Non prenderlo/la (m/f).
Nohn PREHN-dehr-loh/lah.

Don't pick that up.

Apri la porta.
Ah-PREE lah POHR-tah.

Open the door.

Non chiudere la porta.
Nohn KYOO-deh-reh lah POHR-tah.

Don't lock the door.

Non aprire la finestra.
Nohn ah-PREE-reh lah fee-NEHS-trah.

Don't open the window.

Non sporgerti dalla finestra.
Nohn spohr-JEHR-tee DAHL-lah
fee-NEHS-trah.

Don't lean out of the window.

Chiudi il frigorifero.
KYOO-dee eel free-gohr-ee-FEH-roh.

Close the refrigerator.

Metti la scatola là.
MEHT-tee lah SKAH-toh-lah lah.

Put the box over there.

Salta! Non saltare!
SAHL-tah! Nohn sahl-TAH-reh!

Jump! Don't jump!

Rallenta!
Rahl-LEHN-tah!

Slow down!

Non correre. Cammina!
Nohn kohr-REH-reh. Kahm-MEE-nah!

Don't run. Walk!

Non andare troppo svelto.
Nohn ahn-DAH-reh TROHP-poh SVEHL-toh.

Don't hurry.

Inciamperai.
Een-chee-ahm-PEHR-ah-ee.

You'll trip.

Non avere fretta.
Nohn ah-VEH-reh FREHT-tah.

Take your time.

Muoviti!
Mwoh-VEE-tee!

Hurry!

Dobbiamo sbrigarci.
Dohb-bee-AH-moh sbree-GAHR-chee.

We must hurry.

Dobbiamo andare.
Dohb-bee-AH-moh ahn-DAH-reh.

We must go.

Mangia in cucina, così non farai macchie
sul tapeto.
MAHN-jyah een koo-CHEE-nah, koh-ZEE
nohn fah-RAH-ee MAH-kee-eh suhl
tah-PEH-toh.

Eat in the kitchen so you
don't stain the rug.

Non dimenticare di pulirti i piedi.
Nohn dee-mehn-tee-KAH-reh dee
puhl-EER-tee ee pee-EH-dee.

Don't forget to wipe your
feet.

Instructions and Proposals

Metti a posto la scarpa.
MEHT-tee ah POHS-toh lah SKAHR-pah.

Put the shoe back in its place.

Stai indietro.
Stai een-dee-EH-troh.

Stand back.

Non toccare la stufa.
Nohn tohk-KAH-reh lah STOO-fah.

Don't touch the stove.

Ti brucerai.
Tee broo-cheh-RAH-ee.

You will burn yourself.

Ti sei bruciato/a ? (m/f)
Tee say broo-chee-AH-toh/ tah?

Did you burn yourself?

Non giocare con i fiammiferi.
Nohn jyoh-KAH-reh kohn ee
fee-ahm-MEE-feh-ree.

Don't play with matches.

Non andare vicino alle scale.
Nohn ahn-DAH-reh vee-CHEE-noh
AHL-leh SKAH-leh.

Don't go near the stairs.

Non attraversare la strada.
Nohn aht-trah-vehr-SAH-reh lah
STRAH-dah.

Don't cross the street.

Guarda da una parte e dall'altra prima
di attraversare.
GWAHR-dah dah OO-nah PAHR-teh
eh dahl-AHL-trah PREE-mah dee
aht-trah-vehr-SAH-reh.

Look both ways before crossing.

Aspetta la luce verde.
Ahs-PEHT-tah lah LOO-cheh VEHR-deh.

Wait for the green light.

D'ora in poi, fai attenzione.
DOH-rah een POH-ee, fai
aht-tehn-tsee-OH-neh!

From now on, be careful!

Prendilo per il manico.
PREHN-dee-loh pehr eel MAH-nee-koh.

Hold it by the handle.

Prendilo con due mani.
PREHN-dee-loh kohn DOO-eh MAH-nee.

Hold it with two hands.

Fai attenzione a quel che stai facendo.
Fai aht-tehn-tsee-OH-neh ah
kwehl keh stai fah-CHEHN-doh.

Pay attention to what you.
are doing.

Non farlo/la cadere per terra.
Nohn FAHR-loh/lah kah-DEH-reh
pehr TEHR-rah.

Don't drop it on the
ground.

Non tagliarti il dito; il coltello è affilato.
Nohn tah-LYAHR-tee eel DEE-toh;
eel kohl-TEHL-loh eh ahf-fee-LAH-toh.

Don't cut your finger; the
knife is sharp.

Non prenderlo/la.
Nohn prehn-DEHR-loh/lah.

Don't grab that.

...perchè lo dico io.
pehr-KEH loh DEE-koh EE-oh.

... because I say so.

...perchè è così.
pehr-KEH eh koh-ZEE.

... because that's the
way it is.

Per piacere...(portami la scopa?)
Pehr pee-ah-CHEH-reh...(POHR-tah-
mee lah SKOH-pah?)

Could you please...
(bring me the mop?)

Credi che...(potresti aiutarmi
a preparare il pranzo?)
KREH-dee keh...(poh-TREH-stee
ai-oo-TAHR-mee ah preh-pah-RAH-
reh eel PRAHN-tsoh?)

Do you think that...
(you could help me
prepare lunch?)

Credi che potrai...(portare il piatto?)
KREH-dee keh poh-TRAH-ee...
(pohr-TAH-reh eel pee-AHT-toh?)

Do you think that you
can... (carry the dish?)

Posso domandare...(perchè hai gettato il sasso?)
POHS-soh doh-mahn-DAH-reh...(pehr-KEH ai geht-TAH-toh eel SAHS-soh?)

May I ask you...(why you threw that rock?)

Che cosa possiamo fare?
Keh KOH-zah pohs-SYAH-moh FAH-reh?

What can we do?

Proviamo assieme.
Proh-vee-AH-moh ahs-see-EHM-eh.

Let's try together.

Fa salire tuo fratello.
Fah sah-LEE-reh TOO-oh frah-TEHL-loh.

Have your brother come upstairs.

Digli di venire.
DEE-lyee dee veh-NEE-reh.

Tell him to come.

Fa entrare tua sorella.
Fah ehn-TRAH-reh TOO-ah soh-REHL-lah.

Have your sister come in.

Voglio vederlo/la.
VOH-lyoh veh-DEHR-loh/lah.

I want to see him/her.

Hai sporcato la camicia.
Ai spohr-KAH-toh lah kah-MEE-chee-ah.

You have dirtied your shirt.

Vai in camera tua e mettiti un'altra camicia.
Vai een KAH-meh-rah TOO-ah eh MEHT-tee-tee oon AHL-trah kah-MEE-chee-ah.

Go to your room and put on another shirt.

Mostrami dov'è la tua camera.
Moh-STRAH-mee DOH-veh lah TOO-ah KAH-meh-rah.

Show me where your room is.

Che cosa stai facendo?
Keh KOH-zah stai fah-CHEN-doh?

What are you doing/making?

Page - 34

Lasciaglielo fare.
Lah-shee-ah-LYEE-eh-loh FAH-reh.

Let him do it.

Sdraiati.
ZDRAH-ee-ah-tee.

Lie down.

Dondola la bambina con dolcezza.
DOHN-doh-lah lah bahm-BEE-nah
kohn dohl-CHEHTZ-zah.

Rock the baby gently.

Dimmi che cosa è successo.
DEE-mee keh KOH-zah eh soo-CHEHS-soh.

Tell me what happened.

Siediti. Rimani seduto.
SYEH-dee-tee. Ree-MAH-nee seh-DOO-toh.

Sit down. Remain seated.

Alzati. Rimani in piedi.
Ahl-TZAH-tee. Ree-MAH-nee
een pee-EH-dee.

Stand up. Remain stand-ing.

L'hai fatto tu?
Lai FAHT-toh too?

Was it you who did it?

L'hai fatto apposta?
Lai FAHT-toh ahp-POHS-tah?

Did you do it on purpose?

Bada come parli!
BAH-dah KOH-meh PAHR-lee!

Watch your language!

Voglio che mi dica la verità.
VOH-lyoh keh mee DEE-kah lah
vehr-ee-TAH.

I want you to tell me the truth.

Parla più lentamente/chiaro.
PAHR-lah pyoo lehn-tah-MEHN-
teh/ kee-AH-roh.

Speak more slowly/ clearly.

Ascolta attentamente.
Ahs-KOHL-tah aht-tehn-tah-MEHN-teh.

Listen carefully.

Non ti comporti bene oggi.
Nohn tee kohm-POHR-tee BEH-neh
OHJ-jee.

You are not behaving
well today.

Promettimi che ti comporterai bene.
Pro-MEHT-tee-mee keh tee kohm-
POHR-teh-rah-ee BEH-neh.

Promise me to behave.

Comportati bene.
Kohm-pohr-TAH-tee BEH-neh.

Behave yourself.

Comprendi quel che ti dico?
Kohm-PREHN-dee kwehl keh tee
DEE-koh?

Do you understand what
I'm saying?

Non fare il birichino.
Nohn FAH-reh eel bee-ree-KEE-noh.

Don't be naughty.

Sei ostinato/ a! (m/f)
Say oh-stee-NAH-toh/ tah!

Are you stubborn!

Non piangere. Calmati.
Nohn PYAHN-jeh-reh. KAHL-mah-tee.

Don't cry. Calm down.

Non essere nervoso/a. (m/f)
Nohn EHS-seh-reh nehr-VOH-zoh/ zah.

Don't be nervous.

Tutto andrà bene.
TOO-toh ahn-DRAH BEH-neh.

Everything will be all
right.

Mostrami dove ti fa male.
MOHS-trah-mee DOH-veh tee fah
MAH-leh.

Show me where it hurts.

Ti sei fatto male al naso.
Tee say FAHT-toh MAH-leh ahl-NAH-zoh.

You bumped your nose.

Strofinalo con la mano.
Stroh-FEE-nah-loh kohn lah MAH-noh.

Rub it with your hand.

Apri la bocca.
Ah-PREE lah BOHK-kah.

Open your mouth.

Non ti mettere la chiaia in bocca.
Nohn tee MEHT-teh-reh lah KYAH-yah
een BOHK-kah.

Don't put the pebble in
your mouth.

Non far brutte facce.
Nohn fahr BROOT-teh FAHCH-cheh.

Don't make faces.

Ti farà bene.
Tee fah-RAH BEH-neh.

It will do you good.

Soffiati il naso.
SOHF-fee-ah-tee eel NAH-zoh.

Blow your nose.

Respira con il naso.
REHS-pee-rah kohn eel NAH-zoh.

Breathe through your
nose.

Non dirmi che...
Nohn DEER-mee keh...

Don't tell me that...

Hai una risposta per tutto.
Ai OO-nah rees-POHS-tah pehr
TOOT-toh.

You have an answer for
everything.

Dimentica il tuo giocattolo
per un momento.
Dee-MEHN-tee-kah eel TOO-oh
jee-oh-KAHT-toh-loh pehr oon
moh-MEHN-toh.

Forget your toy for a
moment.

Usa i tuoi giocattoli.
OO-zah ee twoy jee-oh-KAHT-toh-lee.

Use your own toys.

Ricordati di portare i tuoi pastelli.
Ree-KOHR-dah-tee dee pohr-TAH-
reh ee twoy pahs-TEHL-lee.

Remember to bring your
crayons.

Instructions and Proposals_____

Portami...   Bring me...
POHR-tah-mee...

Vieni qui con me.   Come here with me.
Vee-EH-nee kwee kohn meh.

Immediatamente.   Immediately.
Eem-meh-dee-ah-tah-MEHN-teh.

Vai al gabinetto.   Go to the bathroom.
Vai ahl gah-bee-NEHT-toh.

Vai per primo.   Go first.
Vai pehr PREE-moh.

Di qui. Seguimi.   This way. Follow me.
Dee kwee. Seh-goo-EE-mee.

Lo puoi fare solo/a? (m/f)   Can you do it yourself?
Loh pwoy FAH-reh SOH-loh/ah?

Non puoi farlo da solo/a?   Can't you do it yourself?
Nohn pwoy FAHR-loh dah SOH-loh/ ah?

Scendi giù e aiuta la nonna.   Go downstairs and help
SHEN-dee jyoo eh ai-OO-tah   grandma.
lah NOHN-nah.

Gioca /di sopra /di sotto.   Play upstairs/downstairs.
Jee-OH-kah/ dee SOHP-rah/ dee SOHT-toh.

Esci. Entra.   Go out. Come in.
EH-shee. EHN-trah.

Vieni! Andiamo!   Come on! Let's go!
Vee-EH-nee! Ahn-dee-AH-moh!

Accendi il registratore.   Turn on the cassette.
Ahch-CHEN-dee eel reh-jees-trah-TOHR-eh.

Abbassa la radio.
Ahb-BAHS-sah lah RAHD-ee-oh.

Lower the radio.

Spegni la televisione.
SPEH-nyee lah teh-leh-vee-zee-OH-neh.

Turn off the television.

Non spegnere la luce.
Nohn SPEH-nyeh-reh lah LOO-cheh.

Don't turn off the light.

Accendila di nuovo.
Ahch-CHEHN-dee-lah dee NWOH-voh.

Turn it on again.

Non riesco a trovare la
strada al buio.
Nohn ree-EHS-koh ah troh-VAH-
reh lah STRAH-dah ahl BOO-yoh.

I can't find my way
in the dark.

Premi/ spingi l'interrutore.
PREH-mee/ SPEEN-jee leen-tehr-
roo-TOH-reh.

Press the switch.

Quello non è tuo. (m)
KWEHL-loh nohn eh TOO-oh.

That's not yours.

Quella non è tua. (f)
KWEHL-lah nohn eh TOO-ah.

That's not yours.

Questo è tuo.
KWEH-sto eh TOO-oh.

This one is yours.

Ecco: il tuo--eel TOO-oh (m/s)

There is yours.

la tua--lah TOO-ah (f/s)

le tue--leh TOO-eh (f/pl)

i tuoi--ee twoy   (m/pl)

BATHROOM ACTIVITIES

The bathroom is an intriguing, splashy place. Lots to do and say here.

Devi andare al gabinetto? DEH-vee ahn-DAH-reh ahl gah-bee-NEHT-toh?	Do you need to go to the bathroom?
Dimmi quando devi andare al gabinetto. DEEM-mee KWAHN-doh DEH-vee ahn- DAH-reh ahl gah-bee-NEHT-toh.	Tell me when you have to go to the bathroom.
Mi hai detto che dovevi andare al gabinetto. Mee ai DEHT-toh keh DOH-veh-vee ahn-DAH-reh ahl gah-bee-NEHT-toh.	You told me that you had to go to the bathroom.
Vai a lavarti. Vai ah lah-VAHR-tee.	Go get washed.
La tua faccia è sporca. Lavala. Lah TOO-ah FACH-chee-ah eh SPOHR-kah. LAH-vah-lah.	Your face is dirty. Wash it.
Non dimenticare di lavarti le mani. Nohn dee-mehn-tee-KAHR-eh dee lah-VAHR-tee leh MAH-nee.	Don't forget to wash your hands.
Ti sei lavato/a il collo? (m/f) Tee say lah-VAH-toh/ tah eel KOHL-loh?	Did you wash your neck?

Page - 40

Pulisciti le unghie.
Poo-LEE-shee-tee leh OON-gee-eh.

Clean your fingernails.

Spazzolati i denti.
Spahtz-TZOH-lah-tee ee DEHN-tee.

Brush your teeth.

Lo spazzolino da denti è sopra
il lavandino.
Loh spahtz-tzoh-LEE-noh dah
DEHN-tee eh SOH-prah eel
lah-vahn-DEE-noh.

Your toothbrush is on the
sink.

Pulisciti dietro le orecchie.
Poo-LEE-shee-tee dee-EH-troh
leh oh-REHK-kee-eh.

Clean behind your ears.

Non ti sei lavato/a la faccia.   (m/f)
Nohn tee SEH lah-VAH-toh/tah
lah FACH-chee-ah.

You didn't wash your
face.

La faccia e le mani sono pulite.
Lah FACH-chee-ah eh leh MAH-nee
SOH-noh poo-LEE-teh.

Your face and hands are
clean.

Ora sei pulito/a.   (m/f)
OH-rah say poo-LEE-toh/ tah.

Now you look clean.

Devi fare il bagno.
DEH-vee FAH-reh eel BAH-nyoh.

You need to take a bath.

Apri il rubinetto.
Ah-PREE eel roo-bee-NEHT-toh.

Turn on the faucet.

Chiudi l'acqua.
KYOO-dee LAH-kwah.

Turn off the water.

Stai facendo il bagno?
Stai fah-CHEN-doh eel BAH-nyoh?

Are you taking a bath?

Bathroom Activities

Sto preparando il bagno per te.
Stoh preh-pahr-AHN-doh eel BAH-
nyoh pehr teh.

I'm running a bath for you.

Vedi come scorre l'acqua?
VEH-dee KOH-meh SKOHR-reh
LAH-kwah?

See the water run?

L'acqua è/ troppo calda/ troppo
fredda/ giusta.
LAH-kwah eh/ TROHP-poh
KAHL-dah/ TROHP-poh FREHD-dah/
JYOOS-tah.

The water is too hot/ too cold/ just right.

Non mettere troppa acqua
nella vasca da bagno.
Nohn MEHT-teh-reh TROHP-pah
AH-kwah NEHL-lah VAHS-kah dah
BAH-nyoh.

Don't fill the tub with too much water.

Ti lavo la schiena, le ginocchia e le dita.
Tee LAH-voh lah skee-EH-nah,
leh jee-NOHK-kyah eh leh DEE-tah.

I'm washing your back knees and toes.

Usa molto sapone.
OO-zah MOHL-toh sah-POH-neh.

Use plenty of soap.

Il sapone ha un buon odore,
però è molto scivoloso.
Eel sah-POH-neh ah oon bwohn
oh-DOH-reh, peh-ROH eh MOHL-toh
shee-voh-LOH-zoh.

The soap smells good, but it is slippery.

Non ti serve tanto sapone.
Nohn tee SEHR-veh TAHN-toh
sah-POH-neh.

You don't need so much soap.

Asciugati bene.
Ah-shee-OO-gah-tee BEH-neh.

Dry yourself well.

Vuota la vasca da bagno.
VWOH-tah lah VAHS-kah dah
BAH-nyoh.

Empty the tub.

Piega l'asciugamano.
Pee-EH-gah lah-shyoo-gah-MAH-noh.

Fold the towel.

Appendi l'assiugamano piccolo.
Ahp-PEHN-dee lah-shyoo-gah-MAH-
noh PEEK-koh-loh.

Hang up the face cloth.

Hai spento la luce?
Ai SPEHN-toh lah LOO-cheh?

Did you turn out the light?

Ti piace fare il bagno?
Tee pee-AH-cheh FAH-reh eel
BAH-nyoh?

Do you like to take a bath?

No. Non mi piace.
Noh. Nohn mee pee-AH-cheh.

No. I don't like it.

GETTING DRESSED

Is it to be the cowboy outfit or the space suit this morning? When you're in a hurry this is not an option, I know. Perhaps, instead, when your little girl dresses dolls herself or your little guy is playing with his action figures, you and they can try some of the phrases in this chapter.

Alzati! È tempo di svegliarsi.
AHL-tsah-tee! Eh TEHM-poh dee
zveh-LYAHR-see.

Get up! It's time to wake up.

Ti cambierò il pannolino.
Tee kahm-bee-eh-ROH eel pahn-
noh-LEE-noh.

I'm changing your diaper.

Metti la mano nella manica.
MEHT-tee lah MAH-noh NEHL-lah
MAH-nee-kah.

Put your hand through the sleeve.

Ti metto la scarpa destra sul piede destro.
Tee MEHT-toh lah SKAHR-pah DEHS-
trah suhl pee-EH-deh DEHS-troh.

I'm putting your right foot into your right shoe.

Hai messo il piede nella scarpa sbagliata.
Ai MEHS-soh eel pee-EH-deh
NEHL-lah SKAHR-pah zbah-LYAH-tah.

You have put your foot in the wrong shoe.

Abbottonati la camicia.
Ab-boht-TOH-nah-tee lah kah-MEE-chee-ah.

Button your shirt.

Vuoi metterti la camicotta blu
o la camicotta rossa?
Vwoy MEHT-tehr-tee lah kah-mee-
KOHT-tah bloo oh lah kah-mee-
KOHT-tah ROHS-sah?

Do you want to wear the
blue blouse or the red
blouse?

Dov'è il tuo cappello?
DOH-veh eel TOO-oh kahp-PEHL-loh?

Where is your hat?

Chiudi la cerniera lampo
della giacca.
KYOO-dee lah chehr-nee-EH-rah
LAHM-poh DEHL-lah jee-AHK-kah.

Close the zipper on your
jacket.

Cerca i tuoi guanti.
Chehr-KAH ee twoy GWAHN-tee.

Look for your gloves.

Devi vestirti da solo/a; (m/f)
la mamma e andata a lavorare.
DEH-vee vehs-TEER-tee dah SOH-loh/
SOH-lah; lah MAHM-mah eh
ahn-DAH-tah ah lah-voh-RAH-reh.

You must dress yourself;
mommy has gone to work.

Vestiti!
VEHS-tee-tee!

Get dressed!

Dobbiamo vestirci.
Dohb-bee-AH-moh vehs-TEER-chee.

We must get dressed

Non mangiarti le unghie.
Nohn mahn-JYAHR-tee leh OON-
gee-eh.

Don't bite your nails.

Mettiti le mutande e i pantaloni.
MEHT-tee-tee leh moo-TAHN-deh eh
ee pahn-tah-LOH-nee.

Put on your underpants and
slacks.

Mettiti il cappotto nuovo.
MEHT-tee-tee eel kahp-POHT-toh
NWOH-voh.

Wear your new coat.

Lascia che ti aiuti ad allacciare
le scarpe.
LAH-shee-ah keh tee ai-YOO-tee ahd
ahl-lach-CHYAH-reh leh SKAHR-peh.

Let me help you tie your
shoe laces.

Hai un laccio annodato della scarpa.
Ai oon LAHCH-chyoh ahn-noh-
DAH-toh DEHL-lah SKAHR-pah.

There's a knot in your
shoe lace.

Pettinati.
PEHT-tee-nah-tee.

Comb your hair.

Spazzolati i capelli.
SPAHTS-tsoh-lah-tee ee kah-PEHL-lee.

Brush your hair.

La spazzola,il pettine e la lima per le
unghie sono sul comò.
Lah SPAHTS-tsoh-lah, eel PEHT-
tee-neh eh lah LEE-mah pehr leh
OON-gee-eh SOH-noh suhl koh-MOH.

The brush, comb and nail
file are on the dresser.

Che bello/ bella che sei!
Keh BEHL-loh/BEHL-lah keh say!

How nice you (m/f) look!

MEALTIME

Put a marker in the "Beverages," "Desserts," "Meats," etc. pages of this book in order to expand your foods vocabulary. You might even want to pretend you and your children are one of the birds from the "Birds" page, and pick some of the "Insects" you might find appetizing. (Something to do AFTER mealtime.)   Buon appetito!

Vuoi fare colazione?
Vwoy FAH-reh koh-lah-tsee-OH-neh?

Do you want breakfast?

Vieni a prendere i tuoi cereali.
Vee-EH-nee ah PREHN-deh-reh ee
twoy cheh-reh-AH-lee.

Come and get your cereal.

Quando pranziamo?
KWAHN-doh prahn-ZYAH-moh?

When are we having lunch?

Che cosa vuoi da mangiare?
Keh KOH-zah vwoy dah mahn-JYAH-reh?

What would you like to eat?

Non hai mangiato niente.
Nohn ai mahn-JYAH-toh nee-EHN-teh.

You have not eaten anything.

Quando mangiamo?
KWAHN-doh mahn-JYAH-moh?

When are we eating?

La cena è pronta. Siediti.
Lah CHEH-nah eh PROHN-tah.
SYEH-dee-tee.

Dinner is ready. Sit down.

Siediti vicino alla tavola.
SYEH-dee-tee vee-CHEE-noh
AHL-lah TAH-voh-lah.

Sit close to the table.

Non mettere i gomiti sopra la tavola.
Nohn MEHT-teh-reh ee GOH-mee-tee
SOH-prah lah TAH-voh-lah.

Don't put your elbows on
on the table.

Vuoi fare un bello spuntino?
Vwoy FAH-reh oon BEHL-loh
spoon-TEE-noh?

Would you like a nice
snack?

Vuoi pancetta o patate?
Vwoy pahn-CHET-tah oh pah-TAH-teh?

Do you want bacon or
potatoes?

Prendi.
PREHN-dee.

Help yourself.

Fatti un panino.
FAHT-tee oon pah-NEE-noh.

Fix yourself a sandwich.

Posso avere più carote?
POHS-soh ah-VEH-reh pyoo kah-ROH-teh?

May I have more carrots?

Ne vuoi ancora?
Neh vwoy ahn-KOH-rah?

Do you want more?

Ne vorresti ancora?
Neh vohr-REHS-tee ahn-KOH-rah?

Would you want more?

Ce n'è ancora per me?
Cheh neh ahn-KOH-rah pehr meh?

Is there any more left
for me?

Prendo ancora un po' di cereali.
PREHN-doh ahn-KOH-rah oon poh
dee cheh-reh-AH-lee.

I'll take a little more
cereal.

Non ne voglio più.
Nohn neh VOH-lyoh pyoo.

I don't want any more.

Puoi passarmi il sale?
Pwoy pahs-SAHR-mee eel
SAH-leh?

Would you pass the salt?

Usa la forchetta, il coltello,
il cucchiaio.
OO-zah lah fohr-KEHT-tah, eel kohl-
TEHL-loh, eel kook-KYAH-yoh.

Use your fork, knife,
spoon.

Non stringere la banana nella mano.
Nohn STREEN-jeh-reh lah bah-
NAH-nah NEHL-lah MAH-noh.

Don't squeeze the banana
in your hand.

Mangia la mela matura, ma fai
attenzione ai semi.
MAHN-jyah lah MEH-lah mah-TOO-rah,
mah fai aht-tehn-tzee-OH-neh
ai SEH-mee.

Eat the ripe apple, but
be careful of the pits.

Lasciami tagliare la tua carne.
LAH-shyah-mee tahl-YAH-reh
lah TOO-ah KAHR-neh.

Let me slice your meat.

C'è qualcuno che vuole un "hot dog"?
Cheh kwahl-KOO-noh keh VWOH-leh
oon "hot dog"?

Would anyone like a "hot dog"?

Non bere il latte così svelto.
Nohn BEH-reh eel LAHT-teh koh-
ZEE ZVEHL-toh.

Don't drink your milk so
fast.

Mangiane solo un poco.
MAHN-jyah-neh SOH-loh oon POH-koh.

Eat just a little.

Il cibo ha un buon odore.
Eel CHEE-boh ah oon bwohn oh-DOH-reh.

The food smells good.

Il caffè è amaro.
Eel kaf-FEH eh ah-MAH-roh.

The coffee is bitter.

Questo budino è troppo dolce.
KWEHS-toh boo-DEE-noh eh
TROHP-poh DOHL-cheh.

This pudding is too sweet.

Il sugo non sa di nulla.
Eel SOO-goh nohn sah dee NUHL-lah.

The sauce is flat.

Il pesce è troppo salato.
Eel PEH-sheh eh TROHP-poh sah-LAH-toh.

The fish is too salty.

La bistecca è al sangue.
Lah bees-TEHK-kah eh ahl SAHN-gweh.

The steak is juicy.

Ti piace il formaggio?
Tee pee-AH-cheh eel fohr-MAHJ-jyoh?

Do you like the cheese?

Vuoi un sorso di tè?
Vwoy oon SORH-soh dee teh?

Would you like a sip of tea?

Mangia gli spinaci.
MAHN-jyah lyee spee-NAH-chee.

Eat your spinach.

Mi piacciono i fagiolini.
Mee pee-AH-chee-oh-noh ee
fah-jyoh-LEE-nee.

I like stringbeans.

Tu puoi mangiare da solo/a. (m/f)
Too pwoy mahn-JYAH-reh dah SOH-loh/lah.

You can feed yourself.

Prova.
PROH-vah.

Try it.

Non parlare con la bocca piena.
Nohn pahr-LAH-reh kohn lah
BOHK-kah pee-EH-nah.

Don't speak with your mouth full.

Che buona cena!
Keh BWOH-nah CHEN-ah!

What a good dinner!

Attento/a a versare il latte nel bicchiere. Aht-TEHN-toh/tah ah vehr-SAH-reh eel laht-teh nehl beek-kee-EH-reh.	Pour the milk carefully into the glass.
Attento/a a tagliare il pane. Aht-TEHN-toh/tah ah tah-LYAH- reh eel PAH-neh.	Cut the bread carefully.
Non riempire il bicchiere. Nohn ree-ehm-PEE-reh eel beek-kee-EH-reh.	Don't fill the glass.
Non versare l'acqua. Nohn vehr-SAH-reh LAH-kwah.	Don't spill the water.
Perchè devi mangiare tanto? Pehr-KEH DEH-vee mahn-JYAH- reh TAHN-toh?	Why must you eat so much?
Finisci il pranzo/cena. Fee-NEE-shee eel PRAHN-zoh/ CHEH-nah.	Finish your lunch/dinner.
Finisci il succo d'arancia. Fee-NEE-shee eel SOOK-koh dah- RAHN-chee-ah.	Finish your orange juice.
Hai finito di mangiare? Ai fee-NEE-toh dee mahn-JYAH-reh?	Have you finished eating?
Tutto finito! TOOT-toh fee-NEE-toh!	All gone!
Hai mangiato tutto quello che c'era sul piatto. Ai mahn-JYAH-toh TOOT-toh KWEHL- loh keh CHEH-rah suhl pee-AHT-toh.	You have eaten everything on your plate.
Buon appetito! Bwohn ahp-peh-TEE-toh!	Enjoy your meal!
Oh! Com' è buono! Oh! KOH-meh BWOH-noh!	Oh! How delicious!

BEDTIME

This is a fine time to read a story or book in Italian to your child. The language he hears before going to sleep will linger in his mind during the night. This might also be a golden opportunity to learn and recite prayers in Italian.

Che sbadiglio!
Keh zbah-DEE-lyoh!

What a yawn!

Stai sbadigliando.
Stai zbah-dee-LYAHN-doh.

You're yawning.

Sei stanco/a? (m/f)
Say STAHN-koh/ kah?

Are you tired?

Hai sonno?
Ai SOHN-noh?

Are you sleepy?

Ti metto a letto.
Tee MEHT-toh ah LEHT-toh.

I'm putting you to bed.

Vuoi che ti metta a letto?
Vwoy keh tee MEHT-tah ah LEHT-toh?

Do you want me to put you bed?

Vai a prendere il tuo libro.
Vai ah PREHN-deh-reh eel TOO-oh
LEE-broh.

Go get your book.

Ti leggerò una storia prima che vai a letto.
Tee lehj-jeh-ROH OO-nah STOH-ree-
ah PREE-mah keh vai ah LEHT-toh.

I'll read you a story
before you go to bed.

Hai il permesso di guardare la televisione?
Ai eel pehr-MEHS-soh dee gwahr-DAH-reh
lah teh-leh-vee-zee-OH-neh?

Do you have permission
to watch television?

Togliti i vestiti.
TOH-lyee-tee ee vehs-TEE-tee.

Take off your clothes.

Mettiti il pigiama.
MEHT-tee-tee eel pee-jee-AH-mah.

Put on your pajamas.

Appendi la camicia alla stanpella.
Ahp-PEHN-dee lah kah-MEE-chee-
ah AHL-lah stahn-PEHL-lah.

Hang your shirt on the
hanger.

Metti via tutti i vestiti.
MEHT-tee VEE-ah TOOT-tee ee
vehs-TEE-tee.

Put all your clothes
away.

Queste calze hanno bisogno di essere
lavate.
KWEHS-teh KAHL-tzeh AHN-noh
bee-ZOH-nyoh dee EHS-seh-reh
lah-VAH-teh.

These socks need
laundering.

Sei pronto/a per andare a letto? (m/f)
Say PROHN-toh/tah pehr ahn-DAH-reh
ah LEHT-toh?

Are you ready for bed?

Di' "Buona notte" al papà.
Dee "BWOH-nah NOHT-teh ahl pah-PAH.

Say,"Goodnight" to Daddy.

Hai detto le preghiere?
Ai DEHT-toh leh preh-ghee-EH-reh?

Did you say your prayers?

Stai diventando pesante.
Stai dee-vehn-TAHN-doh peh-ZAHN-teh.

You're getting heavy.

Chiudi gli occhi. Dormi.
KYOO-dee lyee OHK-kee. DOHR-mee.

Close your eyes. Go to
sleep.

Stai fermo/a... buono/a. (m/f) Stai FEHR-moh/ mah...BWOH-noh/nah.	Be still... quiet.
Sogni d'oro! SOH-nyee DOH-roh!	Pleasant dreams! (Lit: Dreams of gold)
Devi rimanere a letto. DEH-vee ree-mah-NEH-reh ah LEHT-toh.	You must stay in bed.
Devi dormire. DEH-vee dohr-MEE-reh.	You have to sleep.
Non sei ancora a letto? Nohn say ahn-KOH-rah ah LEHT-toh?	You're not in bed yet?
Non è troppo presto per andare a letto. Nohn eh TROHP-poh PREHS-toh pehr ahn-DAH-reh ah LEHT-toh.	It's not too early to go to bed.
Vuoi la luce accesa? Vwoy lah LUH-cheh ah-CHEH-zah?	Do you want the light lit?
La mamma ti vuol bene. Lah MAHM-mah tee vwohl BEH-neh.	Mommy loves you.
Dammi un bacio. DAHM-mee oon BAH-chyoh.	Give me a kiss.
Che Dio ti benedica. Keh DEE-oh tee beh-neh-DEE-kah.	God bless you.
Sei bagnato/a? (m/f) Say bah-NYAH-toh/tah?	Are you wet?
Sei sveglio/a? (m/f) Say SVEH-lyoh/ lyah?	Are you awake?

Dormi?
DOHR-mee?

Are you asleep?

Dorme.
DOHR-meh.

She/he is sleeping.

Perchè non dormi ancora?
Pehr-KEH nohn DOHR-mee ahn-
KOHR-ah?

Why are you not yet
asleep?

Non riesci a dormire?
Nohn ree-EH-shee ah dohr-MEE-reh?

You can't fall asleep?

Non svegliarlo/la.(m/f)
Nohn zveh-LYAHR-loh/lah.

Don't wake him/her.

Che cosa vuoi, piccolo mio?
Keh KOH-zah vwoy, PEEK-koh-
loh MEE-oh?

What do you want my
little one?

Ti sei graffiato/ah la faccia nel sonno.
Tee say grahf-fee-AH-toh /tah lah
FAHCH-chee-ah nehl SOHN-noh.

You scratched your face
in your sleep.

Ti senti male?
Tee SEHN-tee MAH-leh?

Are you sick?

Non ti senti bene?
Nohn tee SEHN-tee BEH-neh?

Don't you feel well?

Ti gira tutto?
Tee JEE-rah TOOT-toh?

Are you dizzy?

Hai la febbre.
Ai lah FEHB-breh.

You have a fever.

Ci sono macchie sul tuo petto.(Varicella)
Chee SOH-noh MAHK-kee-eh suhl
TOO-oh PEHT-toh. (Vah-ree-CHEHL-lah)

There are spots on your
chest. (Chicken pox)

Le tue ghiandole sono gonfie.
Leh TOO-eh GHYAHN-doh-leh
SOH-noh gohn-FEE-eh.

Your glands are swollen.

Tira fuori la lingua.
TEE-rah FWOH-ree lah LEEN-gwah.

Stick out your tongue.

Hai il raffredore.
Ai eel rahf-freh-DOH-reh.

You have a cold.

Hai la tosse.
Ai lah TOHS-seh.

You're coughing.

Avrai bisogno di qualche cosa
per quella tosse.
AH-vrah-ee bee-ZOH-nyoh dee
KWAHL-keh KOH-zah pehr
KWEHL-lah TOHS-seh.

You'll need something for
that cough.

Domani dovrai stare a letto.
Doh-MAH-nee doh-VRAH-ee STAH-reh
ah LEHT-toh.

Tomorrow you'll have to
stay in bed.

Ti fa male il braccio/piede?
Tee fah MAH-leh eel BRACH-choh/
pee-EH-deh?

Does your arm/foot hurt?

Vuoi un nuovo cerotto per il dito?
Vwoy oon NWOH-voh chehr-
OH-toh pehr eel DEE-toh?

Do you want a new
bandaid for your finger?

Hai dormito bene?
Ai dohr-MEE-toh BEH-neh?

Did you sleep well?

Sei ancora stanco/a? (m/f)
Say ahn-KOH-rah STAHN-koh/kah?

Are you still tired?

Ti senti meglio?
Tee SEHN-tee MEH-lyoh?

Do you feel better?

HELPING AT HOME

Your children are happiest when they're imitating adults in their lives. This includes the work they do. You and your children working together is a natural setting for speaking Italian together.

Aiutami ad apparecchiare la tavola.
Ai-YOO-tah-mee ahd ahp-pahr-
rehk-KYAH-reh lah TAH-voh-lah.

Help me set the table.

Puoi mettere la tovaglia e le salviette.
Pwoy MEHT-teh-reh lah toh-VAH-
lyah eh leh sahl-vee-EHT-teh.

You can put on the table-
cloth and napkins.

Apparecchia la tavola per favore.
Ahp-pah-REHK-kyah lah TAH-voh-
lah pehr fah-VOH-reh.

Set the table, please.

Sparecchia la tavola.
Spah-REHK-kyah lah TAH-voh-lah.

Clear the table.

Aiutami a lavare/asciugare i piatti.
Ai-YOO-tah-mee ah lah-VAH-reh/
ah-shyoo-GAH-reh ee pee-AHT-tee.

Help me wash/dry the
dishes.

Aiutami a fare il letto/ pulire
la casa/ fare il bucato.
Ai-YOO-tah-mee ah FAH-reh eel
LEHT-toh/poo-LEE-reh lah KAH-zah/
FAH-reh eel boo-KAH-toh.

Help me make the bed/
clean the house/ do the
wash.

Hai fatto il letto?
Ai FAHT-toh eel LEHT-toh?

Did you make your bed?

L'hai fatto?
Lai FAHT-toh?

Did you do it?

Perchè no?
PEHR-kay noh?

Why not?

Bravo/a.
BRAH-voh/vah.

Good boy/ girl.

Mi fai lavorare.
Mee fai lah-voh-RAH-reh.

You make me work.

La mamma sta spazzando il pavimento.
Lah MAHM-mah stah spatz-TZAHN-
doh eel pah-vee-MEHN-toh.

Mother's sweeping the
floor.

Papà passa l'aspirapolvere sul tappeto.
Pah-PAH PAHS-sah lahs-pee-rah-
POHL-veh-reh suhl tahp-PEH-toh.

Daddy is vacuuming the rug.

L'aspirapolvere fa uno strano rumore.
Lahs-pee-rah-POHL-veh-reh fah
OO-noh STRAH-noh roo-MOH-reh.

The vacuum cleaner makes
a strange noise.

Che polvere! Spolveriamo.
Keh POHL-veh-reh! Spohl-veh-ree-AH-moh.

What dust! Let's dust.

Tieni lo straccio in mano, e
pulisci. Così.
Tee-EH-nee loh STRAHCH-chee-oh
een MAH-noh, eh pool-EE-shee. Koh-ZEE.

Hold the dust cloth in
your hand, and rub. Like
this.

Sto cucendo una gonna per la bambina.
Stoh koo-CHEN-doh OO-nah GOHN-
nah pehr lah bahm-BEE-nah.

I'm sewing a skirt for
the baby.

Aiuta papà a cucinare il pranzo.
Ai-YOO-tah pah-PAH ah koo-chee-
NAH-reh eel PRAHN-tzoh.

Help father cook lunch.

La mamma sta facendo una torta.
Lah MAHM-mah stah fah-CHEN-doh
OO-nah TOHR-tah.

Mother's baking a cake.

Vuoi aiutarmi a fare i biscotti?
Vwoy ai-yoo-TAHR-mee ah
FAH-reh ee bee-SKOHT-tee?

Do you want to help me
bake some cookies?

Versa la farina.
VEHR-sah lah fah-REE-nah.

Pour in the flour.

Frullo le uova.
FRUHL-loh leh oo-OH-vah.

I'm beating the eggs.

Sto mischiando lo zucchero e
il burro.
Stoh mees-kee-AHN-doh loh DZOOK-
keh-roh eh eel BOOR-roh.

I'm mixing the sugar and
the butter.

Ci occorre lievito?
Chee ohk-KOHR-reh
lee-EH-vee-toh?

Do we need baking powder?

Li cuciniamo nel forno.
Lee koo-chee-NYAH-moh nehl
FOHR-noh.

We bake them in the oven.

Regola l'orologio per mezz'ora.
REH-goh-lah loh-roh-LOH-jee-oh
pehr mehdz-DZOH-rah.

Set the clock for one-
half hour.

I biscotti sono fatti.
Ee bees-KOHT-tee SOH-noh FAHT-tee.

The cookies are done.

Non puoi aiutarmi a stirare.
Nohn pwoy ai-yoo-TAHR-mee
ah stee-RAH-reh.

You cannot help me iron.

Mi puoi aiutare a dividere e piegare
la biancheria.
Mee pwoy ai-yoo-TAH-reh ah
dee-VEE-deh-reh eh pee-eh-GAH-reh
lah bee-ahn-keh-REE-ah.

You can help me sort and
fold the laundry.

Dopo aver pulito, potremo
leggere una storia.
DOH-poh ah-VEHR poo-LEE-toh,
poh-TREH-moh LEHJ-jeh-reh
OO-nah STOH-ree-ah.

After cleaning, we can
read a story.

Prima di giocare, devi
riordinare la tua camera.
PREE-mah dee jyoh-KAH-reh,
DEH-vee ree-ohr-dee-NAH-reh
lah TOO-ah KAH-meh-rah.

Before playing, you must
straighten your room.

Vuoi venire a fare la spesa con me?
Vwoy veh-NEE-reh ah FAH-reh
lah SPEH-zah kohn meh?

Would you like to go
(food) shopping with me?

È necessario comprare qualcosa
da mangiare.
Eh neh-chehs-SAH-ree-oh kohm-
PRAH-reh kwahl-KOH-zah dah
mahn-JYAH-reh.

We need to buy something
to eat.

Hai bisogno di nuovi vestiti.
Ai bee-ZOH-nyoh dee NWOH-vee
vehs-TEE-tee.

You need new clothes.

Dobbiamo spalare la neve.
Dohb-bee-AH-moh spah-LAH-reh
lah NEH-veh.

We need to shovel the
snow.

Aiutami a tagliare l'erba del prato.
Ai-YOO-tah-mee ah tah-LYAH-reh
LEHR-bah dehl PRAH-toh.

Help me cut the lawn.

Pianta i semi in fila.
Pee-AHN-tah ee SEH-mee een FEE-lah.

Plant the seeds in a row.

Ci sono così tante erbacce!
Chee SOH-noh koh-ZEE TAHN-teh
EHR-bahch-cheh!

There are so many weeds!

Dobbiamo ripulire il giardino dalle
erbacce, così le piante riescono crescere.
Dohb-bee-AH-moh ree-poo-LEE-reh
eel jyahr-DEE-noh DAHL-leh EHR-bahch-
cheh, koh-ZEE leh pee-AHN-teh
ree-EHS-koh-noh KREH-sheh-reh.

We need to weed the
garden so that the plants
can grow.

Vuoi aiutarmi ad annaffiare il giardino?
Vwoy ai-yoo-TAHR-mee ahd
ahn-nahf-fee-AH-reh eel jyahr-DEE-noh?

Will you help me water
the garden?

Non scavare troppo!
Nohn skah-VAH-reh TROHP-poh!

Don't dig too much!

Scavalo qui.
SKAH-vah-loh kwee.

Dig here.

Stai attento/a ai bruchi. (m/f)
Stai aht-TEHN-toh/ tah ai BROO-kee.

Be careful of the
caterpillars.

Puoi rastrellare le foglie?
Pwoy rahs-trehl-LAH-reh leh FOH-lyee-eh?

Can you rake the leaves?
(as a favor)

Getta le foglie nel secchio
dell'immondizia.
JEHT-tah leh FOH-lyee-eh nehl SEHK-
kee-oh dehl-leem-mohn-DEE-tzee-ah.

Throw the leaves into the
garbage bag.

Non puoi potare gli alberi.
Nohn pwoy poh-TAH-reh lyee
AHL-beh-ree.

You cannot prune the trees.

È troppo pericoloso.
Eh TROHP-poh peh-ree-koh-LOH-zoh.

It's too dangerous.

Invece di potare, puoi aiutarmi
a fare un carrettino.
Een-VEH-cheh dee poh-TAH-reh,
pwoy ai-yoo-TAHR-mee ah
FAH-reh oon kahr-reht-TEE-noh.

Instead of pruning, you can help me make a wagon.

Puoi strofinare con la carta
vetrata questo pezzo di legno?
Pwoy stroh-fee-NAH-reh kohn
lah KAHR-tah veh-TRAH-tah KWEHS-
toh PEHTZ-tzoh dee LEH-nyoh?

Can you sand this piece of wood?

Sega questa tavola in due.
SEH-gah KWEHS-tah TAH-voh-lah
een DOO-eh.

Saw this board in two.

Dammi il cacciavite.
DAHM-mee eel kahch-chee-ah-
VEE-teh.

Give me the screwdriver.

Pianta questo chiodo con
il martello.
Pee-AHN-tah KWEHS-toh kee-OH-doh
kohn eel mahr-TEHL-loh.

Hammer this nail with the hammer.

Vuoi guardare?
Vwoy gwahr-DAH-reh?

Do you want to watch?

SHOPPING

This is the area of foreign language conversation which may be temperamental. When children are little you can speak Italian to them without restraint. However, as children grow more sensitive among other people they may not wish to appear "different" i.e., speaking a foreign language that others might overhear. Assure them that you will not embarrass them if that's how they feel, and resume speaking Italian outside the store or in the car. Perhaps you might suggest to them that you and they "play store" at home using Italian. You can get plenty of ideas from all the stores listed below.

Vuoi venire a fare acquisti?
Vwoy veh-NEE-reh ah FAH-reh
ahk-KWEES-tee?

Do you want to go shopping?

Vuoi venire con me:
Vwoy veh-NEE-reh kohn meh:

Do you want to come with me:

al deposito di legname,
ahl deh-POH-dzee-toh dee
leh-NYAH-mee,

to the lumber yard,

al negozio di ferramenta,
ahl neh-GOH-tzee-oh dee
fehr-rah-MEHN-tah,

to the hardware store,

al vivaio,
ahl vee-VAH-ee-oh,

to the nursery,

al distributore di benzina,
ahl dees-tree-boo-TOH-reh
dee behn-TZEE-nah,

to the gas station,

all'aeroporto, ahl-ah-eh-roh-POHR-toh,	to the airport,
al porto, ahl POHR-toh,	to the marina,
al fornaio, ahl fohr-NAH-ee-oh,	to the bakery,
alla drogheria, AHL-lah droh-geh-REE-ah,	to the grocery store,
alla lavanderia, AHL-lah lah-vahn-deh-REE-ah,	to the laundrymat,
al mercato, ahl mehr-KAH-toh,	to the market,
ai grandi magazzini, ai GRAHN-dee mah-gahdz-DZEE-nee,	to the department store,
alla farmacia, AHL-lah fahr-mah-CHEE-ah,	to the drug store,
alla macelleria, AHL-lah mah-chehl-leh-REE-ah,	to the butcher's shop,
alla banca, AHL-lah BAHN-kah,	to the bank,
alla biblioteca, AHL-lah bee-blee-oh-TEH-kah,	to the library,
alla calzoleria, AHL-lah kahl-tzoh-leh-REE-ah,	to the shoe store,
al calzolaio, ahl kahl-tzoh-LAH-ee-oh?	to the shoemaker?

Sto andando al mercato.
Stoh ahn-DAHN-doh ahl
mehr-KAH-toh.

I am going to the market.

Devo comprare...
DEH-voh kohm-PRAH-reh...

I need to buy...

Devo rendere...
DEH-voh REHN-deh-reh...

I have to return...
(give something back)

C'è una svendita.
Cheh OO-nah zvehn-DEE-tah.

There's a sale.

Cosa comprerai con il tuo dollaro?
KOH-zah kohm-preh-RAI kohn
eel TOO-oh dohl-LAH-roh?

What will you buy with
your dollar?

Prendiamo l'ascensore/ la scala mobile.
Prehn-DYAH-moh lah-shehn-SOH-
reh/ lah SKAH-lah MOH-bee-leh.

Let's take the elevator/
escalator.

Puoi sederti nel carrello.
Pwoy seh-DEHR-tee nehl kahr-REHL-loh.

You can sit in the
shopping cart.

Stai nel carrello.
Stai nehl kahr-REHL-loh.

Stay in the cart.

Metti i piedi nelle fessure.
MEHT-tee ee pee-EH-dee NEHL-leh
fehs-SOO-reh.

Put your feet through
the openings.

Non possiamo spendere troppo. Nohn pohs-SYAH-moh SPEHN-deh-reh TROHP-poh.	We cannot spend too much (money).
Non possiamo comprarlo. Nohn pohs-SYAH-moh kohm-PRAHR-loh.	We cannot buy that.
È troppo costoso. Eh TROHP-poh kost-OH-zoh.	That's much too expensive.
Forse qualcosa di più economico. FOHR-seh kwal-KOH-zah dee pyoo eh-koh-NOH-mee-koh.	Perhaps something cheaper.
Sono a corto di soldi. SOH-noh ah KOHR-toh dee SOHL-dee.	I'm short of money.
Il commesso/ La commessa/ è laggiù. Eel kohm-MEHS-soh/Lah kohm-MEHS-sah/ eh LAHJ-jyoo.	The salesman/saleswoman is over there.
Quant'è? KWAHN-teh?	How much is it?
Quanto costa? KWAHN-toh KOHS-tah?	How much does it cost?
Lo compriamo? Loh kohm-PRYAH-moh?	Shall we buy it?
Qual è la taglia di questo cappotto? Kwahl eh lah TAHL-yah dee KWEHS-toh kahp-POHT-toh?	What size is this coat?
Fammelo vedere. FAH-meh-loh veh-DEH-reh.	Let me see that.

Provalo.
PROH-vah-loh.

Try it on.

È troppo aderente/abbondante.
Eh TROHP-poh ah-deh-REHN-teh/
ahb-bohn-DAHN-teh.

This is too tight/loose.

È troppo grande/ piccolo.
Eh TROHP-poh GRAHN-deh/
PEEK-koh-loh.

This is too large/small.

Ti sta bene addosso.
Tee stah BEH-neh ahd-DOHS-soh.

It looks good on you.

Controlla il resto.
Kohn-TROHL-lah eel REH-stoh.

Count your change.

Non toccarlo.
Nohn tohk-KAHR-loh.

Don't touch that.

Hai bisogno di andare al bagno?
Hai bee-ZOHN-yoh dee ahn-DAH-
reh ahl BAHN-yoh?

Do you need to go to the
bathroom?

EXCLAMATIONS ! ! !

Ah! Formidabile!
Ah! Fohr-mee-DAH-bee-leh!

Ah! Wow!

Ahi!
AY-ee!

Ouch!

Sono triste.
SOH-noh TREES-teh.

I'm sad.

Son contento/a. (m/f)
SOHN kohn-TEHN-toh/ tah.

I'm glad.

Siamo contenti che avete vinto!
See-AH-moh kohn-TEHN-tee keh
ah-VEH-teh VEEN-toh!

We're glad that you won!

Aiuto!
Ai-YOO-toh!

Help!

Attenzione!
Aht-tehn-tsee-OH-neh!

Look out! Watch out!

Mi dispiace. È colpa mia.
Mee dee-spee-AH-cheh. Eh KOHL-
pah MEE-ah.

I'm sorry. It's my fault.

Mi dispiace che tu sia caduto/a. (m/f)
Mee dees-pee-AH-cheh keh too
SEE-yah kah-DOO-toh/ tah.

I'm sorry that you fell.

Allora!
Ahl-LOH-rah!

Well now!

Non è così?
Nohn eh koh-ZEE?

Isn't that so?

Chi se ne importa!
Kee seh neh eem-POHR-tah!

Who cares!

Non me ne importa!
Nohn meh neh eem-POHR-tah!

I don't care!

Non è importante.
Nohn eh eem-pohr-TAHN-teh.

It doesn't matter.

Chi sa?
Kee sah?

Who knows?

Vai piano!
Vai pee-AH-noh!

Go easy!

Va bene.
Vah BEH-neh.

O.K. All right.

Naturalmente.
Nah-too-rahl-MEHN-teh.

Of course.

Niente affatto!
NYEHN-teh ahf-FAHT-toh!

Of course not!

Certamente.
Cher-tah-MEHN-teh.

Certainly.

Sicuro!
See-KOO-roh!

Sure!

Indubbiamente.
Een-doob-byah-MEHN-teh.

Without fail.

Che interessante! Keh een-teh-rehs-SAHN-teh!	How interesting!
Che comico! Keh KOH-mee-koh!	How funny!
Che sciocchezza! Keh shee-OHK-keh-tsah!	What nonsense!
Che fortuna! Keh fohr-TOO-nah!	What luck!
Sei fortunato. Say fohr-too-NAH-toh.	You're lucky.
Che terribile! Keh tehr-REE-bee-leh!	How awful!
Che peccato! Keh pehk-KAH-toh!	Too bad! What a pity!
Che insolito! Keh een-SOH-lee-toh!	How unusual!
Quello è straordinario! KWEHL-loh eh strah-ohr-dee- NAH-ree-oh!	That's extraordinary!
Che gentile/simpatico! Keh jehn-TEE-leh/seem-PAH-tee-koh!	How kind/ nice!
Meraviglioso! Meh-rah-vee-LYOH-zoh!	Marvelous! Wonderful!
Che scherzo! Keh SKEHR-tzoh!	What a joke!
Spero. Spero di no. SPEH-roh. SPEH-roh dee noh.	I hope so. I hope not.

Credo. Credo di no. KREH-doh. KREH-doh dee noh.	I think so. I think not.
È fuori di scussione! Eh FWOH-ree dee skoos-SEE-oh-neh!	It's out of the question!
Non preoccuparti. Nohn preh-ohk-koo-PAHR-tee.	Don't worry.
Calmati. KAHL-mah-tee.	Relax. Be quiet.
Puo succedere a chiunque. Pwoh sooch-CHEH-deh-reh ah KYOON-kway.	It could happen to anyone.
Va bene. Vah BEH-neh.	It's all right.
Non è giusto. Nohn eh JYOOS-toh.	It's not right.
Non è necessario. Nohn eh neh-chehs-SAH-ree-oh.	That's not necessary.
Finito! Fee-NEE-toh!	All gone!
Up-la! OOP-lah!	Up you go!
Che disordine! Keh dees-OHR-dee-neh!	What a mess!
È vero. Eh VEH-roh.	That's true.

Veramente?
Veh-rah-MEHN-teh?

Is that so?

Bene...Allora Fammi vedere...
BEH-neh...Ahl-LOH-rah...
FAHM-mee veh-DEH-reh...

Well...Then...Let me see.
(An expression of hesitation while considering a reply.)

Ebbene!
Ehb-BEH-neh!

Well now!

Davvero! Ma non mi dire!
Dahv-VEH-roh!
Mah nohn mee DEE-reh!

Indeed! You don't say!

Come al solito...
KOH-meh ahl soh-LEE-toh...

As usual...

Che starnuto! Salute!
Keh stahr-NOO-toh! Sah-LOO-teh!

What a sneeze! God bless you!

Che broncio!
Keh BROHN-chyoh!

What a frown!

Che non va?
Keh nohn vah?

What's wrong?

Che cosa ti succede?
Keh KOH-zah tee sooch-CHEH-deh?

What's the matter with you?

Di che cosa ti lamenti?
Dee keh KOH-zah tee lah-MEHN-tee?

Why are you complaining?

Perchè piangi?
Pehr-KEH pee-AHN-jee?

Why are you crying?

Guarda!
GWAHR-dah!

Look!

Per l'amor di Dio!
Pehr lah-MOHR-dee DEE-oh!

For goodness sake!

Che stupido sono stato!
Keh STOO-pee-doh SOH-noh
STAH-toh!

How stupid of me!

Questo non è un scherzo!
KWEHS-toh nohn eh oon
SKEHR-tsoh!

This is no laughing matter!

Te lo meriti!
Teh loh meh-REE-tee!

It serves you right!

Non devi dirlo.
Nohn DEH-vee DEER-loh.

You must not say that.

Che Dio ti perdoni!
Keh DEE-oh tee pehr-DOH-nee!

God forbid!

Per l'amor del cielo!
Pehr lah-MOHR dehl chee-EH-loh!

Why on earth!

È immenso!
Eh eem-MEHN-soh!

It's immense!

Va bene!
Vah BEH-neh!

That's fine!

Page - 73

GREETINGS

Pronto! PROHN-toh!	Hello! (On the telephone)
Chi parla? Kee PAHR-lah?	Who's speaking? (On the telephone)
Buon giorno. Buona giornata. Bwohn JYOHR-noh. BWOH-nah jyohr-NAH-tah.	Good morning. Good day.
Ciao. Come va? Chyow. KOH-meh vah?	Hello. How goes it?
Buona sera. BWOH-nah SEH-rah.	Good evening.
Ti sono mancato? Tee SOH-noh mahn-KAH-toh?	Did you miss me?
Abbracciami. Ahb-BRAHCH-chya-mee.	Give me a hug.
Dammi un bacio. DAHM-mee oon BAH-chyoh.	Give me a kiss.
Come stai? KOH-meh stai?	How are you?
Molto bene. Grazie. MOHL-toh BEH-neh. GRAH-tzee-eh.	Very well. Thank you.

Così-così.
Koh-ZEE-koh-ZEE.

So-so.

Buona notte.
BWOH-nah NOHT-teh.

Good night.

Arrivederci.
Ahr-ree-veh-DEHR-chee.

Good-bye.

Ciao. A presto.
Chyow. Ah PREHS-toh.

So long. See you soon.

Scusami.
SKOO-sah-mee.

Excuse me.

Che Dio ti benedica.
Keh DEE-oh tee beh-neh-DEE-kah.

God bless you.

Salute!
Sah-LOO-teh!

To your health!
(Toast or sneeze)

Buon compleanno!
Bwohn kohm-pleh-AHN-noh!

Happy Birthday!

Buon Natale!
Bwohn nah-TAH-leh!

Merry Christmas!

Buon Anno!
Bwohn AHN-noh!

Happy New Year!

Per piacere.
Pehr pee-ah-CHEH-reh.

Please.

Grazie.   Prego.
GRAH-tzee-eh. PREH-goh.

Thank you. You're
welcome.

Benvenuto!
Behn-vehn-OO-toh!

Welcome!

PRAISE

All the ways to say, "You're tops!" "None better!" "Wonderful, Wonderful you!" and many, many more. Use this chapter OFTEN. You and your child will love it.

Che bella voce!
Keh BEHL-lah VOH-cheh!

What a beautiful voice!

Tu cammini/disegni/parli/canti/ balli/ bene.
Too kahm-MEE-nee/dee-SEH-nyee/
pahr-lee/KAHN-tee/BAHL-lee/
BEH-neh.

You walk/ draw/ speak/ sing/ dance/ well.

Come mangi/scrivi/nuoti/giochi/ bene.
KOH-meh MAHN-jee/ SKREE-vee/
NWOH-tee/ jee-OH-kee/ BEH-neh.

How well you eat/ write/ swim / play.

Sei meraviglioso/a. (m/f)
Say meh-rah-vee-lyee-OH-zoh/ah.

You're wonderful.

Sei brillante!
Say breel-LAHN-teh!

You're brilliant!

Come sei dolce.
KOH-meh say DOHL-cheh.

How sweet you are.

Come sei carino/a, bello/a, forte,
corraggioso/a. (m/f)
KOH-meh say kahr-EE-noh/ nah, BEHL-
loh/ lah, FOHR-teh, kohr-ahj-JYOH-zoh/zah.

How cute, handsome/
pretty, strong, brave
you are.

Questo vestito ti sta bene.
KWEHS-toh vehs-TEE-toh tee
stah BEH-neh.

This dress suits you well.

Che begli occhi hai.
Keh BEH-lyee OHK-kee ai.

What pretty eyes you have.

Mi piacciono i tuoi occhi/ le tue mani/
e il tuo pancino.
Mee pee-AHCH-chee-oh-noh ee twoy
OHK-kee/ leh TOO-eh MAH-nee/
eh eel TOO-oh pahn-CHEE-noh.

I love your eyes/ your hands/ and your tummy.

Che bei riccioli.
Keh BEH-ee REE-chee-oh-lee.

What pretty curls.

Che buona ragazza!
Keh BWOH-nah rah-GAHTZ-tzah!

What a good girl!

Che buon ragazzo!
Keh bwohn rah-GAHTZ-tzoh!

What a good boy!

Come sei simpatico/a! (m/f)
KOH-meh say seem-PAH-tee-koh/kah!

How nice you are!

Sei così simpatico/a. (m/f)
Say koh-ZEE seem-PAH-tee-koh/ kah.

That's nice of you.

Sei di buon umore.
Say dee bwohn oo-MOH-reh.

You are in good spirts.

Mi piaci.
Mee pee-AH-chee.

I like you.

Ti amo.
Tee AH-moh.

I love you.

Bravo.
BRAH-voh.

Bravo. Well done.

Praise

È corretto. Eh kohr-REHT-toh.	That's correct.
Mi piace come giochi, in silenzio da solo/a. Mee pee-AH-cheh KOH-meh JYOH-kee, een see-LEHN-tsyoh dah SOH-loh/lah.	I like the way you play quietly by yourself.
Continua a provare. Non smettere. Kohn-TEE-noo-ah ah proh-VAH-reh. Nohn SMEHT-teh-reh.	Keep trying. Don't give up.
Che magnifica idea! Keh mah-NYEE-fee-kah ee-DEH-ah!	What a magnificent idea!
Diventi sempre più bravo. Dee-VEHN-tee SEHM-preh pyoo BRAH-voh.	You're getting better and better.
Certamente mi è piaciuto il tuo aiuto. Cher-tah-MEHN-teh mee eh pee-ah-chee-OO-toh eel TOO-oh ai-YOO-toh.	I certainly liked your help.
Hai pulito la tua camera. Ai poo-LEE-toh lah TOO-ah KAH-meh-rah.	You cleaned your room.
Tu sei stato/stata paziente quando io parlavo al telefono. Too say STAH-toh/STAH/tah pah-tzee-EHN-teh KWAHN-doh EE-oh pahr-LAH-voh ahl teh-LEH-foh-noh.	You were (m/f) patient while I was talking on the telephone.

BIRTHDAY PARTY

Che cosa vuoi per il tuo compleanno?
Keh KOH-zah vwoy pehr
eel TOO-oh kohm-pleh-AHN-noh?

What would you like for your birthday?

Vorresti fare una festa?
Vohr-REH-stee FAH-reh OO-nah
FEHS-tah?

Would you like to have a party?

Inviteremo i tuoi amici.
Een-vee-teh-REH-moh ee twoy ah-MEE-chee.

We'll invite your friends.

Avremo torta, gelato, cappelli,
giochi e regali.
Ah-VREH-moh TOHR-tah, jeh-
LAH-toh, kahp-PEHL-lee,
jee-OH-kee eh reh-GAH-lee.

We'll have cake, ice cream, hats, games and presents.

Chi vorresti invitare?
Kee vohr-REH-stee een-vee-TAH-reh?

Whom would you like to invite?

Vuoi fare la festa a casa, in un
ristorante, al parco o alla spiaggia?
Vwoy FAH-reh lah FEHS-tah

Would you like to have the party at home, in a restaurant , at the park,

ah KAH-zah, een oon rees-toh-
RAHN-teh, ahl PAHR-koh, oh
AHL-lah spee-AHJ-jee-ah?

or at the beach?

Quanti anni hai?
KWAHN-tee AHN-nee ai?

How old are you?

Ho cinque anni.
Oh CHEEN-kweh AHN-nee.

I am five years old.

Non so.
Nohn soh.

I don't know.

Spengi le candele.
SPEHN-jee leh kahn-DEH-leh.

Blow out the candles.

Taglia la torta.
TAH-lyah lah TOHR-tah.

Cut the cake.

Dividi la torta in otto pezzi.
Dee-VEE-dee lah TOHR-tah een
OHT-toh PEHTS-tsee.

Divide the cake into
eight pieces.

Che bella festa!
Keh BEHL-lah FEHS-tah!

What a nice party!

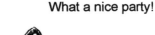

PLAYING

If this chapter's pages don't have paint stains, water marks, tire tracks and gum still sticking the pages together, you're not getting all there is to wring out of these pages! Be sure to write in some additional sentences and expressions you've learned elsewhere that are appropriate. I've found it helpful to put up 3 x 5-card size sentences and phrases wherever I need them until the phrase is part of my thinking.

Cucù. Sèttete.
Koo-KOO. SEHT-teh-teh.

Peek-a-boo.

Indovina chi è?
Een-doh-VEE-nah kee eh?

Guess who?

Non puoi giocare con le biglie
in cucina.
Nohn pwoy jyoh-KAH-reh kohn
leh BEEL-yeh een koo-CHEE-nah.

You cannot play with
your marbles in the
kitchen.

Sei libero/a di andar fuori giocare.
Say LEE-beh-roh/rah dee ahn-DAHR
FWOH-ree jyoh-KAH-reh.

You are free to go out
and play.

Puoi invitare i tuoi amici di scuola.
Pwoy een-vee-TAH-reh ee
twoy ah-MEE-chee dee skoo-OH-lah.

You may invite your
school friends.

Domanda loro se vogliono
giocare a:
Doh-MAHN-dah LOH-roh seh VOH-
lyoh-noh jyoh-KAH-reh ah:

Ask them if they want to
play:

dottore e infermiera,
doht-TOH-reh eh een-fehr-MEE-eh-rah,

doctor and nurse,

negozio,
neh-GOH-tzee-oh,

store,

mamma e papà,
MAHM-mah eh pah-PAH,

mother and father,

con le bambole,
kohn leh BAHM-boh-leh,

dolls,

campana.
kahm-PAH-nah.

hopscotch.

AIRPLANES

Pilota alla torre di controllo.
Pee-LOH-tah AHL-lah TOHR-reh
dee kohn-TROHL-loh.

Pilot to control tower.

Sto rullando.
Stoh rool-LAHN-doh.

I'm taxiing.

Sto decollando.
Stoh deh-kohl-LAHN-doh.

I'm taking off.

Possiamo atterrare?
Pohs-SYAH-moh aht-tehr-RAH-reh?

May we land?

Siamo senza benzina!
SYAH-moh SEHN-tzah behn-DZEE-nah!

We're out of gas!

Su che pista d'atteraggio possiamo
atterrare?
Soo keh PEES-tah daht-teh-RAJ-
jee-oh pohs-SYAH-moh aht-tehr-RAH-reh?

On which runway may we
land?

ANIMALS

La mia proboscide è lunga; sono
grande; e cammino così. Che
animale sono?
Lah MEE-ah proh-BOH-shee-deh eh
LOON-gah; SOH-noh GRAHN-deh; eh
kahm-MEE-noh koh-ZEE. Keh ah-
nee-MAH-leh SOH-noh?

My trunk is long; I'm
large; and I walk like
this. What animal am I?

Io ho due gobbe; e mi metto a
terra così. Che animale sono?
EE-oh oh DOO-eh GOHB-beh; eh mee
MEHT-toh ah TEHR-rah koh-ZEE.
Keh ah-nee-MAH-leh SOH-noh?

I have two humps; and I
lie down like this. What
animal am I?

Io abbaio e ringhio. Che animale sono?
EE-oh ahb-BAH-ee-oh eh REEN-gee-
oh. Keh ah-nee-MAH-leh SOH-noh?

I bark and growl. What
animal am I?

Facciamo finta di essere canguri.
Saltiamo.
Fah-CHYAH-moh FEEN-tah dee EH-
seh-reh kahn-GOO-ree. Sahl-tee-AH-moh.

Let's pretend we're kan-
garoos. Let's hop.

Facciamo finta di essere galli.
Facciamo una cantata di gallo.
Cu-cu-ru-cu.
Fah-CHYAH-moh FEEN-tah dee EH-
seh-reh GAHL-lee.
Fah-CHYAH-moh OO-nah kahn-TAH-tah
dee GAHL-loh. Koo-koo-roo-koo.

Let's pretend we're
roosters. Let's crow.
Cock-a-doodle-do.

AUTOMOBILES

L'automobile è senza benzina. Lah-oo-toh-MOH-bee-leh eh SEHN-tzah behn-DZEE-nah.	The car is out of gas.
Non funziona più. Nohn foon-tzee-OH-nah pyoo.	It doesn't go anymore.
Perchè non funziona l'automobile? Pehr-KEH nohn foon-tzee-OH-nah lah-oo-toh-MOH-bee-leh?	Why doesn't the car go?
Spingi l'automobile. SPEEN-jee lah-oo-toh-MOH-bee-leh.	Push the car.
Riempitela del tutto. Ree-ehm-PEE-teh-lah dehl TOOT-toh.	Fill her up.
Verificate l'olio, l'acqua e la batteria. Veh-ree-fee-KAH-teh LOH-lee-oh, LAH-kwah eh lah baht-teh-REE-ah.	Check the oil, water and battery.
Guida l'automobile nel autorimessa. GWEE-dah lah-oo-toh-MOH-bee-leh nehl ah-oo-toh-ree-MEHS-sah.	Drive the car into the garage.

BACKYARD

Vai fuori/dentro a giocare. Vai FWOH-ree/DEHN-troh ah jyoh-KAH-reh.	Go outside/inside and play.
Giocate nel cortile/nella cassa di sabbia. Jyoh-KAH-teh nehl kohr-TEE-leh/NEHL-lah KAHS-sah dee SAHB-bee-ah.	Play in the yard/ in the sandbox.

Vuoi fare le bolle di sapone?
Vwoy FAH-reh leh BOHL-leh
dee sah-POH-neh?

Do you want to blow
bubbles?

Non giocare nell'immondizia.
Nohn jyoh-KAHR-reh nehl-leem-
mohn-DEE-tzee-ah.

Don't play in the dirt.

Non cogliere i fiori.
Nohn KOH-lyeh-reh ee fee-OH-ree.

Don't pick the flowers.

Puoi nuotare nell piscina se io sono
con te.
Pwoy nwoh-TAH-reh nehl pee-SHEE-nah
seh EE-oh SOH-noh kohn teh.

You can swim in the pool
if I am with you.

Salta dal trampolino come ti ho
mostrato.
SAHL-tah dahl trahm-poh-LEE-noh
KOH-meh tee oh mohs-TRAH-toh.

Jump off the diving board
as I showed you.

Fai attenzione quando ti arrampichi
sugli alberi.
Fai aht-tehn-tzee-OH-neh
KWAHN-doh tee ahr-RAHM-pee-kee
SOO-lyee AHL-beh-ree.

Be careful climbing
trees.

Tutti due potete sedere nel carro.
C'è abbastanza posto per due.
TOOT-tee DOO-eh poh-TEH-teh
seh-DEH-reh nehl KAHR-roh. Cheh
ahb-bahs-TAHN-tzah POHS-toh
pehr DOO-eh.

Both of you can sit in the
wagon. There's room
enough for two.

Non lasciare il cortile.
Nohn lahs-shee-AH-reh eel kohr-TEE-leh.

Don't leave the yard.

BASEBALL

Acchiappa/tira la palla. Ahk-kee-AHP-pah/TEE-rah lah PAHL-lah.	Catch/throw the ball.
Agguanta la mazza dietro di te. Ahg-GWAHN-tah lah MAHTZ-zah dee-EH-troh dee teh.	Hold the bat behind you.
Non perdere di vista la palla. Nohn PEHR-deh-reh dee VEES-tah lah PAHL-lah.	Keep your eye on the ball.
Oscilla! (la mazza) Oh-SHEEL-lah!(lah MAHTZ-zah)	Swing! (the bat)
Hai fatto un colpo a vuoto.(la palla) Ai FAHT-toh oon KOHL-poh ah VWOH-toh. (lah PAHL-lah)	You missed. (the ball)
Colpisci la palla molto bene. Kohl-PEESH-shee lah PAHL-lah MOHL-toh BEH-neh.	You hit the ball very well.

BICYCLING

Metti il piede sul pedale. MEHT-tee eel pee-EH-deh suhl peh-DAH-leh.	Put your foot on the pedal.
Prova a tenerti in equilibrio. PROH-vah ah teh-NEHR-tee een eh-kwee-LEEB-ryoh.	Try to keep your balance.
Agguanta il manubrio. Ahg-GWAHN-tah eel mah-NOOB-ree-oh.	Hold onto the handlebars.

Stai vicino alla bicicletta.
Stai vee-CHEE-noh AHL-lah
bee-chee-KLEHT-tah.

Stand next to the
bicycle.

Vai dritto; gira a destra/ sinistra.
Vai DREET-toh; JEE-rah ah
DEH-strah/ see-NEE-strah.

Go straight; steer right/
left.

Continua a pedalare.
Kohn-TEE-noo-ah ah peh-dah-LAH-reh.

Keep pedaling.

Guidi la bicicletta molto bene.
GWEE-dee lah bee-chee-KLEHT-tah
MOHL-toh BEH-neh.

You're riding your
bicycle very well.

Suona il campanello.
SWOH-nah eel kahm-pahn-EHL-loh.

Ring the bell.

Non andare in strada con la
bicicletta. C'è troppo traffico.
Nohn ahn-DAH-reh een STRAH-
dah kohn lah bee-chee-KLEHT-tah.
Cheh TROHP-poh TRAHF-fee-koh.

Don't ride your bicycle
in the street. There's
too much traffic.

Vai troppo veloce. Frena!
Vai TROHP-poh veh-LOH-cheh.
FREH-nah!

You're going too fast.
Put on the brakes!

Ti sei fatto male?
Tee say FAHT-toh MAH-leh?

Did you hurt yourself?

BOARD GAMES

Di chi è la mossa?
Dee kee eh lah MOHS-sah?

Whose move is it?

Tocca a te.
TOHK-kah ah teh.

It's your turn. (to play)

Il tuo pezzo è nel punto sbagliato.
Eel TOO-oh PEHTZ-tzoh eh nehl
POON-toh zbah-LYAH-toh.

Your piece is in the
wrong place.

Quello non è un gioco lecito.
KWEHL-loh nohn eh oon JYOH-koh
LEH-chee-toh.

That's not playing fair.

Muovi avanti.
MWOH-vee ah-VAHN-tee.

Move forward.

Muovi indietro.
MWOH-vee een-dee-EH-troh.

Move backward.

Hai vinto.
Ai VEEN-toh.

You won.

Hai perso.
Ai PEHR-soh.

You lost.

Vuoi giocare di nuovo?
Vwoy jyoh-KAH-reh dee NWOH-voh?

Do you want to play again?

BOATS

Tutti a bordo! TOO-tee ah BOHR-doh!	All aboard! (ship)
Facciamo vela per l'Italia. Fahch-chee-AH-moh VEH-lah pehr lee-TAH-lee-ah.	We're sailing for Italy.
La barca affonda. Uomo in mare! Lah BARH-kah ahf-FOHN-dah. Oo-OH-moh een MAH-reh!	The boat is sinking. Man overboard!
Abbandonate la nave! Ahb-bahn-doh-NAH-teh lah NAH-veh!	Abandon ship!
Abassate le scialuppe di salvataggio! Ah-bahs-SAH-teh leh shee-ah- LOOP-peh dee sahl-vah-TAHJ-jyoh!	Lower the life boats!
Ci mettiamo in bacino. Chee meht-tee-AH-moh een bah-CHEE-noh.	We're docking.

BODY PARTS

Con che cosa:	With what:
--corri? (le gambe) --KOHR-ree? (leh GAHM-beh)	--do you run? (legs)
--parli? (la bocca) --PAHR-lee? (lah BOHK-kah)	--do you speak? (mouth)
--vedi? (gli occhi) --VEH-dee? (lyee OHK-kee)	--do you see? (eyes)
--stai in punta di piedi? (dita del piede) --stai een POON-tah dee pee- --EH-dee? (DEE-tah dehl pee-EH-deh)	--do you stand on tip- toe (toes)

COLORING

Lasciala usare i tuoi pastelli.
LAH-shyah-lah oo-ZAH-reh ee
twoy pahs-TEHL-lee.

Let her use your crayons.

Colora il sole di giallo.
Koh-LOH-rah eel SOH-leh dee JAHL-loh.

Color the sun yellow.

Dipingi l'uccello del colore che ti piace.
Dee-PEEN-jee looch-CHEHL-loh dehl
koh-LOH-reh keh tee pee-AH-cheh.

Paint the bird the color
you like.

Disegna il cerchio, triangolo,
il quadrato come questo.
Dee-SEH-nyah eel CHEHR-kyoh,
tree-AHN-goh-loh, eel kwah-DRAH-toh
KOH-meh KWEHS-toh.

Draw the circle, tri-
angle, square like this.

Taglia questa illustrazione dalla rivista.
TAH-lyah KWEHS-tah eel-loos-trah-
tzee-OH-neh DAH-lah ree-VEE-stah.

Cut out this picture from
the magazine.

Incollala con cura sulla carta.
Een-kohl-LAH-lah kohn KOO-rah
SUHL-lah KAHR-tah.

Paste it carefully on the
paper.

Piega la carta in due/ in quatro.
Pee-EH-gah lah KAHR-tah een DOO-
eh/ een KWAH-troh.

Fold the paper in two/ in
four.

Non stracciare la carta.
Nohn strahch-chee-AH-reh lah
KAHR-tah.

Don't tear the paper.

Arrotola /forma /modella l'argilla così.
Ahr-ROH-toh-lah/ FOHR-mah/moh-
DEHL-lah lahr-JEEL-lah koh-ZEE.

Roll/ form/ squeeze the
clay like this.

Pulisci i pastelli e la carta.
Poo-LEE-shee ee pahs-TEHL-lee
eh lah KAHR-tah.

Clean up your crayons
and paper.

DOLLS

Dai da mangiare alla bambola.
Dai dah mahn-JYAH-reh AHL-lah
BAHM-boh-lah.

Feed the doll.

Vesti la bambola.
VEHS-tee lah BAHM-boh-lah.

Dress the doll.

Mettila giù piano.
MEHT-tee-lah jyoo pee-AH-noh.

Lay her down gently.

Non trascinarla sul pavimento.
Nohn trah-shee-NAHR-lah suhl
pah-vee-MEHN-toh.

Don't drag her on the
floor.

Non sculacciarla così forte.
Nohn skoo-lah-chee-AHR-lah
koh-ZEE FOHR-teh.

Don't spank her so hard.

Come si chiama la bambola?
KOH-meh see kee-AH-mah lah
BAHM-boh-lah?

What's the doll's name?

FIRE ENGINES

Aiuto! Fuoco!
Ai-YOO-toh! FWOH-koh!

Help! Fire!

Chiamate i pompieri.
Kee-ah-MAH-teh ee pohm-pee-EH-ree.

Send for the fire
engines.

Suonate la sirena!
Swoh-NAH-teh lah see-REH-nah!

Sound the siren!

FISHING

Dov'è un buon posto per pescare? DOH-veh oon bwohn POHS-toh pehr pehs-KAH-reh?	Where is a good spot for fishing?
La mia lenza è impigliata sul fondo. Lah MEE-ah LEHN-dzah eh eem- peel-YAH-tah suhl FOHN-doh.	My line is caught on the bottom.
Vuoi andare a pescare? Vwoy ahn-DAH-reh ah pehs-KAH-reh?	Would you like to go fishing?

FOLLOW THE LEADER

Io sono il capo. Fate quello che faccio io. EE-oh SOH-noh eel KAH-poh. FAH- teh KWEHL-loh keh FAHCH-chee-oh EE-oh.	I'm the leader. Do what I do.

HIDE-AND-SEEK

Vai a nasconderti. Vai ah nahs-KOHN-dehr-tee.	Go and hide.
Dove sei? DOH-veh say?	Where are you?
Dove sono? DOH-veh SOH-noh?	Where am I?
Ti prenderò. Tee prehn-deh-ROH.	I'm going to get you. (chasing)
Preso! PREH-zoh!	"Gotcha!"

OBSTACLE GAMES

Vai: Go:
Vai:

    oltre il cerchio,   through the hoop,
    OHL-treh eel CHER-kee-oh,

    intorno all'armadio,   around the cabinet,
    een-TOHR-noh ahl-lahr-MAH-dyoh,

    sotto al tavolo,   under the table,
    SOHT-toh ahl TAH-voh-loh,

    vicino al sedia.   beside the chair.
    vee-CHEE-noh ahl SEH-dee-ah.

Stai dietro di me,   Stand behind me,
Stai dee-EH-troh dee meh,

    davanti al divano.   in front of the couch.
    dah-VAHN-tee ahl dee-VAH-noh.

PLAYGROUND

Dondola! Però non dondolare troppo   Swing! But don't swing
forte.   too high.
DOHN-doh-lah! Peh-ROH nohn
dohn-doh-LAH-reh TROHP-poh FOHR-teh.

Non saltare dell'altalena.   Don't jump off the swing.
Nohn sahl-TAH-reh dehl-lahl-tah-LEH-nah.

Non spingere troppo forte.   Don't push too hard.
Nohn SPEEN-jeh-reh TROHP-poh
FOHR-teh.

Non stare in piedi sull'altalena.
Nohn STAH-reh een pee-EH-dee
suhl-lahl-tah-LEH-nah.

Don't stand on the swing.

Ti spingerò piano.
Tee speen-jeh-ROH pee-YAH-noh.

I'll push you gently.

Non chiudere gli occhi.
Nohn KYOO-deh-reh lyee OHK-kee.

Don't close your eyes.

Tieniti alla toboga.
TYEH-nee-tee AHL-lah toh-BOH-gah.

Hold onto the slide.

Scendi piano.
SHEHN-dee pee-YAH-noh.

Slide down easily.

L'aquilone sta cadendo; non c'è
abbastanza vento.
Lah-kwee-LOH-neh stah kah-DEHN-
doh; nohn cheh ahb-bahs-TAHN-tzah
VEHN-toh.

The kite is falling;
there's not enough wind.

Agguanta la coda.
Ahg-GWAHN-tah lah KOH-dah.

Hold onto the tail.

Vuoi saltare la corda o giocare con
la trottola?
Vwoy sahl-TAH-reh lah KOHR-dah
oh jyoh-KAH-reh kohn lah TROHT-
toh-lah?

Do you want to jump rope
or play with the top?

Tira le biglie nel cerchio.
TEE-rah leh BEEL-yeh nehl
CHEHR-kyoh.

Shoot the marbles into
the circle.

Gonfia il pallone. Perde aria.
GOHN-fee-ah eel pahl-LOH-neh.
PEHR-deh AH-ree-ah.

Blow up the balloon. Air
is leaking from it.

PUZZLES

Mettiamo questo pezzo del puzzle qui.
Meht-tee-AH-moh KWEHS-toh
PEHTS-tsoh dehl POOH-zehl kwee.

Let's put this piece of the
puzzle here.

Questo pezzo non si adatta.
KWEHS-toh PEHTS-tsoh nohn see
ah-DAHT-tah.

This piece doesn't fit.

Che pezzo manca?
Keh PEHTS-tsoh MAHN-kah?

Which piece is missing?

SKATING

I miei pattini sono rovinati.
Devono essere affilati.
Ee mee-EH-ee paht-TEE-nee SOH-
noh roh-vee-NAH-tee. Deh-VOH-noh
EHS-seh-reh ahf-fee-LAH-tee.

My skates are dull. They
need to be sharpened.

Tieniti a me. Ti aiuterò a pattinare.
TYEH-nee-tee ah meh. Tee ai-
yoo-teh-ROH ah paht-tee-NAH-reh.

Hold onto me. I'll help
you skate.

Alza il piede destro.
AHL-tzah eel pee-EH-deh DEHS-troh.

Lift your right foot.

Spingi con il piede sinistro.
SPEEN-jee kohn eel pee-EH-deh
see-NEES-troh.

Push with your left foot.

Pattina intorno alla pista di pattinaggio.
PAHT-tee-nah een-TOHR-noh AHL-lah
PEES-tah dee paht-tee-NAHJ-jee-oh.

Skate around the rink.

Sei pronto a pattinare all'indietro.
Say PROHN-toh ah paht-tee-NAH-
reh ahl-leen-dee-EH-troh.

You're ready to skate
backwards.

Pattina solamente nel viale d'accesso.
PAHT-tee-nah soh-lah-MEHN-teh
nehl vee-AH-leh dahch-CHEHS-soh.

Skate only in the drive-.
way.

SOCCER

Non toccare la palla con le mani.
Nohn tohk-KAH-reh lah PAHL-lah
kohn leh MAH-nee.

Don't touch the ball with
your hands.

Calcia la palla nella porta.
KAHL-chee-ah lah PAHL-lah
NEHL-lah POHR-tah.

Kick the ball into the
goal.

Hai fatto un gol!
Ai FAHT-toh oon gohl!

You have scored a goal!

TRAINS

Tutti a bordo!
TOOT-tee ah BOHR-doh!

All aboard! (train)

Biglietti, per piacere.
Bee-lyee-EHT-tee, pehr
pee-ah-CHEH-reh.

Tickets, please.

Quanto è la tariffa?
KWAHN-toh eh lah tah-REEF-fah?

How much is the fare?

Quando arriviamo a New York?
KWAHN-doh ahr-ree-vee-AH-moh
ah New York?

When do we arrive in
New York?

TRUCKS

Distribuisci olio nel tuo camion di olio?
Dees-tree-boo-EE-shee OH-lee-
oh nehl TOO-oh kah-mee-OHN dee
OH-lee-oh?

Are you delivering oil
in your oil truck?

Questo non è un camion per l'olio;
questo è un camion per bestiame.
KWEHS-toh nohn eh oon kah-mee-OHN
pehr LOH-lee-oh.
KWEHS-toh eh oon kah-mee-OHN
pehr behs-tee-AH-meh.

This isn't an oil truck;
this is a cattle truck.

Carico il mio camion di sabbia.
KAH-ree-koh eel MEE-oh kah-mee-
OHN dee SAHB-bee-ah.

I'm loading my truck with
sand.

POTPOURRI

Scuoti il sonaglio.
SKWOH-tee eel soh-NAH-lyoh.

Shake the rattle.

Ammucchia i mattoncini uno
sopra l'altro.
Ahm-MOOK-kyah ee maht-tohn-
CHEE-nee OO-noh SOHP-rah LAHL-troh.

Stack the blocks on top
of each other.

Non gettarli giù.
Nohn jeht-TAHR-lee jyoo.

Don't knock them down.

Dov'è il fazzoletto?
(Nascondi il fazzoletto)
DOH-veh eel fahts-tsoh-LEHT-toh?
(Nahs-KOHN-dee eel fahts-tsoh LEHT-toh)

Where's the handkerchief?
(Hide-the-handkerchief)

Giocha a mosca cieca?
Jee-OH-kah ah MOHS-kah chee-EH-kah?

Are you gong to play
blindman's buff?

Guarda fuori dalla finestra.
GWAHR-dah FWOH-ree DAH-lah
fee-NEHS-trah.

Look out the window.

Che cosa vedi?
Keh KOH-zah VEH-dee?

What do you see?

Io scorgo con il mio piccolo
occhio una cosa che è bruna e
alta...(un albero).
EE-oh SKOHR-goh kohn eel
MEE-oh PEEK-koh-loh OHK-kee-oh
OO-nah KOH-zah keh eh BROO-nah
eh AHL-tah...(oon AHL-beh-roh).

I spy with my little eye
something that is brown
and tall...(a tree).

Rotola il cerchio/ la palla.
ROH-toh-lah eel CHER-kee-oh/
lah PAHL-lah.

Roll the hoop/ the ball.

Vuoi giocare a carte con me?
Vwoy jyoh-KAH-reh ah
KAHR-teh kohn meh?

Do you want to play cards
with me?

END OF PLAY

Basta giocare.
BAH-stah jyoh-KAH-reh.

Stop playing.

È ora di cena.
Eh OH-rah dee CHEH-nah.

It's time for dinner.

Metti in ordine la tua camera.
MEHT-tee een OHR-dee-neh lah
TOO-ah KAH-meh-rah.

Tidy up your room.

Metti tutti i tuoi giocattoli nella cassa dei giocattoli.
MEHT-tee TOOT-tee ee twoy jyoh-KAHT-toh-lee NEHL-lah KAHS-sah day jyoh-KAHT-toh-lee.

Put all your toys back in the toy box.

Dove hai lasciato il tuo pagliaccio?
DOH-veh ai lah-shee-AH-toh eel TOO-oh pah-lyee-AHCH-chee-oh?

Where did you leave your clown?

Vuoi fare una passeggiata?
Vwoy FAH-reh OO-nah pahs-sehj-JYAH-tah?

Do you want to go for a walk?

Preferisci fare un giro?
Preh-feh-REE-shee FAH-reh oon JEE-roh?

Would you prefer to take a ride?

Tieniti alla carrozzina.
TYEH-nee-tee AHL-lah kahr-rotz-TZEE-nah.

Hold onto the carriage.

AT THE BEACH

Any fun situation is excellent learning grounds for lots of new vocabulary and practice for already-learned phrases and expressions. And the beach is such a place. An extra bonus is to let your imagination take you to the Italian Riviera. Sand...water... sunshine...Italian...Why not?

Andiamo alla spiaggia.
Ahn-dee-AH-moh AHL-lah
spee-AHJ-jee-ah.

Let's go to the beach.

Andiamo a riva/ al lago/ nell'oceano.
Ahn-dee-AH-moh ah REE-vah/
ahl LAH-goh/ nehl-oh-CHEH-ah-noh.

Let's go to the shore/ to the lake/ ocean.

Mettiti il costume da bagno giallo.
MEHT-tee-tee eel kohs-TOO-meh
dah BAH-nyoh JAHL-loh.

Put on your yellow bathing suit.

Porteremo con noi gli asciugamani,
la coperta, e la sedia per la spiaggia.
Pohr-teh-REH-moh kohn NOH-ee lyee
ah-shyoo-gah-MAH-nee, lah koh-PEHR-tah,
eh lah SEH-dee-ah pehr lah spee-AHJ-jee-ah.

We're bringing towels, the blanket, and the beach chair.

Il secchiello e la paletta sono nello stanzino.
Eel sehk-KYEHL-loh eh lah pah-
LEHT-tah SOH-noh NEHL-loh stahn-
TZEE-noh.

Your pail and shovel are in the closet.

Incarta i panini e la frutta.
Een-KAHR-tah ee pah-NEE-nee
eh lah FROOT-tah.

Wrap up the sandwiches and the fruit.

Siamo qui! Siamo arrivati.
See-AH-moh kwee! See-AH-moh
ahr-ree-VAH-tee!

Here we are! We have arrived!

Restiamo qui. Non ci sono molte persone.
Rehs-tee-AH-moh kwee. Nohn chee
SOH-noh MOHL-teh pehr-SOH-neh.

Let's stay here. There aren't too many people.

Preferisco l'ombra.
Preh-feh-REES-koh LOHM-brah.

I prefer the shade.

È vicino all'acqua.
Eh vee-CHEE-noh ahl-LAHK-kwah.

It's near the water.

È vicino al chiosco delle bevande.
Eh vee-CHEE-noh ahl KYOHS-koh
DEHL-leh beh-VAHN-deh.

It's near the drink stand.

L'acqua è chiara.
LAHK-kwah eh kee-AH-rah.

The water looks clear.

Guarda le onde!
GWAHR-dah leh OHN-deh!

Look at the waves!

Il mare è mosso.
Eel MAH-reh eh MOHS-soh.

The sea is rough.

L'acqua è calda/ fredda/ rinfrescante. LAHK-kwah eh KAHL-dah/ FREH-dah/ reen-frehs-KAHN-teh.	The water is warm/ cold/ refreshing.
Andiamo a nuotare. Ahn-dee-AH-moh ah nwoh-TAH-reh.	Let's go swimming.
Nuota là vicino al bagnino. NWOH-tah lah vee-CHEE-noh ahl bah-NYEE-noh.	Swim over there near the lifeguard.
Prendi il salvagente. PREHN-dee eel sahl-vah-JEHN-teh.	Take your flotation.
Non puoi andare nell'acqua ora. Hai appena pranzato. Nohn pwoy ahn-DAH-reh nehl-LAHK-kwah OH-rah. Ai ahp-PEH-nah prahn-TZAH-toh.	You can't go in the water now. You've just eaten lunch.
Perchè non raccogli conchiglie? Pehr-KEH nohn rahk-KOH-lyee kohn-KEE-lyee-eh?	Why don't you collect seashells?
Quella lancia è assai vicina alla boa. KWEHL-lah LAHN-chah eh ahs-SAI vee-CHEE-nah AHI-lah BOH-ah.	That speed boat is very close to the buoy.
Andiamo a sciare sull'acqua. Ahn-dee-AH-moh ah shee-AH-reh suhl-LAHK-kwah.	Let's go water skiing.

Galleggia sulla schiena.
Gahl-LEHJ-jee-ah SUHL-lah skee-EH-nah.

Float on your back.

Vieni fuori dall'acqua.
Vee-EH-nee FWOH-ree dahl-LAHK-kwah.

Come out of the water.

Tremi dal freddo.
TREH-mee dahl FREHD-doh.

You're shivering with cold.

Ci sono alghe sulla tua schiena.
Chee SOH-noh AHL-geh SUHL-lah TOO-ah skee-EH-nah.

There's seaweed on your back.

Costruisci un castello di sabbia.
Kohs-troo-EE-shee oon kahs-TEHL-loh dee SAHB-bee-ah.

Build a sand castle.

Non sederti al sole troppo a lungo.
Nohn seh-DEHR-tee ahl SOH-leh TROHP-poh ah LOON-goh.

Don't sit in the sun too long.

Non devi prendere una scottatura.
Nohn DEH-vee PREHN-deh-reh OO-nah skoht-tah-TOO-rah.

You must not get sun-burnt.

Dov'è la lozione abbronzante?
DOH-veh lah loh-tzee-OH-neh ahb-brohn-ZAHN-teh?

Where is the suntan lotion?

Voglio abbronzarmi.
VOH-lyoh ahb-brohn-ZAHR-mee.

I want to get a suntan.

Il sole è forte/ caldo.
Eel SOH-leh eh FOHR-teh/KAHL-doh.

The sun is strong/ hot.

Guarda gli uccelli atterrare/
volare.
GWAHR-dah lyee ooch-CHEHL-lee
aht-tehr-RAH-reh/ voh-LAH-reh.

Watch the birds land/fly.

Hai dimenticato gli occhiali da sole?
Ai dee-mehn-tee-KAH-toh lyee
ohk-KYAH-lee dah SOH-leh?

Did you forget your sun
glasses?

È ora di andare.
Eh OH-rah dee ahn-DAH-reh.

It's time to go.

Prepariamoci.
Preh-pahr-YAH-moh-chee.

Let's pack up.

Mi son divertito/a alla spiaggia. (m/f)
Mee sohn dee-vehr-TEE-toh/ tah
AHL-lah spee-AHJ-jee-ah.

I had a good time at
the beach.

Divertitevi.
Dee-vehr-TEE-teh-vee.

Have a good time.

È divertente andare alla spiaggia.
Eh dee-vehr-TEHN-teh ahn-DAH-
reh AHL-lah spee-AHJ-jee-ah.

It's fun to go to the
beach.

SKIING

Skiing, like other fun activities, is a memorable way to absorb Italian. This time you can imagine yourself and your family in the Italian Alps. Look and listen for Italian opportunities.

Che bella giornata sciare. Keh BEHL-lah jyohr-NAH-tah shee-AH-reh.	What a beautiful day for skiing.
Dobbiamo noleggiare racchette da sci/ sci/ scarponi da sci. Dohb-bee-AH-moh noh-lehj-jee-AH-reh rahk-KEHT-teh dah shee/ shee/ skahr-POH-nee dah shee.	We need to rent ski poles/ skiis/ boots.
Sono comodi i scarponi da sci? SOH-noh KOH-moh-dee ee skahr-POH-nee dah shee?	Are your boots comfortable?
Sono troppo lunghe/ corte le racchette da sci? SOH-noh TROHP-poh LOON-geh/ KOHR-teh leh rahk-KEHT-teh dah shee?	Are your ski poles too long/ short?

I tuoi attacchi sono troppo lenti/ stretti.
Ee twoy aht-TAHK-kee SOH-noh TROHP-poh LEHN-tee/ STREHT-tee.

Your bindings are too loose / tight.

Dove vendono i biglietti per la seggiovia?
DOH-veh VEHN-doh-noh ee bee-lyee-EHT-tee pehr lah sej-jee-oh-VEE-ah?

Where do they sell tickets for the ski lift?

Non andare fino in cima.
Nohn ahn-DAH-reh FEE-noh een CHEE-mah.

Don't go to the top.

Quella collina è un poco ripida.
KWEHL-lah kohl-LEE-nah eh oon POH-koh REE-pee-dah.

That hill is a little steep.

Quegli sciatori fanno una corsa troppo veloce.
KWEH-lyee shee-ah-TOH-ree FAHN-noh OO-nah KOHR-sah TROHP-poh veh-LOH-cheh.

Those skiers race too fast.

Attenzione!
Aht-tehn-tzee-OH-neh!

Look out!

Non sciare troppo forte.
Nohn shee-AH-reh TROHP-poh FOHR-teh.

Don't ski too fast.

La neve è troppo molle/ dura.
Lah NEH-veh eh TROHP-poh MOHL-leh / DOO-rah.

The snow is too soft / hard.

Che forma!
Keh FOHR-mah!

What form!

Tu stai sciando bene.
Too stai shee-AHN-doh BEH-neh.

You are skiing just fine.

Sei stanco/ a? (m/f)
Say STAHN-koh/ kah?

Are you tired?

Hai fame/ freddo?
Ai FAH-meh / FREHD-doh?

Are you hungry/ cold?

Andiamo dentro per riposare/
mangiare/ riscaldarci.
Ahn-dee-AH-moh DEHN-troh pehr
ree-poh-SAH-reh/ mahn-JYAH-reh/
rees-kahl-DAHR-shee.

Let's go inside to rest/
to eat/ to warm up.

Vieni a riscaldarti.
Vee-EH-nee ah rees-KAHL-dahr-tee.

Come and warm up.

È bello e caldo qui.
Eh BEHL-loh eh KAHL-doh kwee.

It's nice and warm here.

Quando partiremo?
KWAHN-doh pahr-tee-REH-moh?

When are we leaving?

WEATHER

"Everybody talks about it..." So the saying goes. Now you and your child can talk about it in Italian! Try sharing a picture book on weather with your child and discuss the pictures using Italian. This could be more of a "school" kind of chapter if you and your child want to play school. Flash cards to make, maps to draw, temperatures to record... Fun to be had!

C'è luce. Cheh LOO-cheh.	It's light.
Che bella giornata! Keh BEHL-lah jyohr-NAH-tah!	What a beautiful day!
Non ci sono nuvole. Nohn chee SOH-noh NOO-voh-leh.	There are no clouds.
Il sole splende. Eel SOH-leh SPLEHN-deh.	The sun is shining.
Fa caldo oggi. Fah KAHL-doh OHJ-jee.	It's hot today.
Il caldo è terribile; è l'estate. Eel KAHL-doh eh tehr-REE-bee-leh; eh lehs-TAH-teh.	It's terribly hot; it's summer.
Abbiamo un'invasione di caldo. Ahb-bee-AH-moh oon-een-vah-zee-OH-neh dee KAHL-doh.	We're having a heat wave.

Non c'è un alito di vento.
Nohn cheh oon AH-lee-toh dee VEHN-toh.

There's not a breath of wind.

Tira vento.
TEE-rah VEHN-toh.

It's windy.

Che bella notte.
Keh BEHL-lah NOHT-teh.

What a beautiful night.

Fa un po' fresco/freddo.
Fah oon poh' FREHS-koh/ FREHD-doh.

It's a little cool/ cold.

Avrai bisogno di un cappotto/ una maglia.
Ahv-RAH-ee bee-ZOH-nyoh dee oon
kahp-POHT-toh/OO-nah MAH-lyee-ah.

You need a coat/ sweater.

È nuvoloso.
Eh noo-voh-LOH-zoh.

It's cloudy.

Piove (a catinelle).
Pee-OH-veh(ah kah-tee-NEHL-leh).

It's raining (cats and dogs).

Guarda la pioggia.
GWAHR-dah lah pee-OHJ-jee-ah.

Look at the rain.

La strada è piena di pozzanghere.
Lah STRAH-dah eh pee-EH-nah dee
pohts-TSAHN-gheh-reh.

The street is full of puddles.

Levati le scarpe.
LEH-vah-tee leh SKAHR-peh.

Take off your shoes.

I tuoi piedi sono bagnati.
EE twoy pee-EH-dee SOH-noh
bah-NYAH-tee.

Your shoes are wet.

Che brutta giornata!
Keh BROOT-tah jyohr-NAH-tah!

What an unpleasant day!

Che tempo terribile!
Keh TEHM-poh tehr-REE-bee-leh!

What awful weather!

Che cattivo tempo!
Keh kaht-TEE-voh TEHM-poh!

What nasty weather!

Il tempo è brutto.
Eel TEHM-poh eh BROOT-toh.

The weather is bad.

Fa scuro.
Fah SKOO-roh.

It's getting dark.

Il cielo è nero / grigio.
Eel chee-EH-loh eh NEH-roh/
GREE-jee-oh.

The sky is dark/gray.

Farà scuro presto.
Fah-RAH SKOO-roh PREHS-toh.

It will be dark soon.

Tuona e fulmina.
Too-OH-nah eh fool-MEE-nah.

There's thunder and
lightening.

Che tempesta!
Keh tehm-PEHS-tah!

What a storm!

Che brutto tempo!
Keh BROOT-toh TEHM-poh!

What a storm!

Che nebbia!
Keh NEHB-bee-ah!

What fog!

Aspetta finche la pioggia
termina.
Ahs-PEHT-tah feen-KEH lah
pee-OHJ-jee-ah TEHR-mee-nah.

Wait until the rain
stops.

Guarda l'arcobaleno.
GWAHR-dah lahr-koh-bah-LEH-noh.

See the rainbow.

È una vera giornata d'inverno.
Eh OO-nah VEHR-ah jyohr-NAH-tah
deen-VEHR-noh.

It's a real winter day.

Sta iniziando a nevicare.
Stah een-eetz-YAHN-doh ah
neh-vee-KAH-reh.

It's beginning to snow.

Nevica.
NEH-vee-kah.

It's snowing.

Cadono fiocchi di neve.
KAH-doh-noh FYOHK-kee dee NEH-veh.

Snow flakes are falling.

Guarda la neve.
GWAHR-dah lah NEH-veh.

Look at the snow.

Come scintilla la neve!
KOH-meh sheen-TEEL-lah lah
NEH-veh!

How the snow sparkles!

Forse possiamo fare un pupazzo di neve.
FOHR-seh pohs-SYAH-moh FAH-reh
oon poo-PAHTZ-zoh dee NEH-veh.

Perhaps we can build a
snowman.

Ha smesso di piovere/ nevicare.
Ah SMEHS-soh dee pee-OH-veh-reh/
neh-vee-KAH-reh.

The rain /snow has
stopped.

La neve si sta sciogliendo.
Lah NEH-veh see stah shyohl-YEHN-doh.

The snow is melting.

TIME

È l'una.
Eh LOO-nah.

It's one o'clock.

Sono le due.
SOH-noh leh DOO-eh.

It's two o'clock.

Sono le tre e quindici (un quarto).
SOH-noh leh treh eh KWEEN-
dee-chee (oon KWAHR-toh).

It's three fifteen.

Sono le quattro e mezza.
SOH-noh leh KWAHT-troh eh MEHDZ-dzah.

It's four thirty.

Sono le quattro e quaranta cinque.
SOH-noh leh KWAHT-troh eh
kwah-RAHN-tah CHEEN-kway.

It's four forty-five.

Sono le sei e venti.
SOH-noh leh say eh VEHN-tee.

It's six twenty.

Sono le sei e quaranta.
SOH-noh leh say eh kwah-RAHN-tah.

It's six forty.

Sono le otto.
SOH-noh leh OHT-toh.

It's eight o'clock.

Sono le nove.
SOH-noh leh NOH-veh.

It's nine o'clock.

Sono le dieci.
SOH-noh leh dee-EH-chee.

It's ten o'clock.

Sono le undici.
SOH-noh leh OON-dee-chee.

It's eleven o'clock.

È mezzanotte.
Eh MEHDZ-dzah-NOHT-teh.

It's midnight.

È mezzogiorno.
Eh MEHDZ-dzoh-JYOHR-noh.

It's noon.

È mattina.
Eh maht-TEE-nah.

It's morning.

È pomeriggio.
Eh poh-mehr-EEJ-jyoh.

It's afternoon.

È notte.
Eh NOHT-teh.

It's night.

È presto. È tardi.
Eh PREHS-toh. Eh TAHR-dee.

It's early. It's late.

Un attimo
Oon AHT-tee-moh

A short while

Il più presto possibile
Eel pyoo PREHS-toh pos-SEE-bee-leh

As soon as possible

QUANTITIES

Che età hai tu?
Keh eh-TAH ai too?

How old are you?

Quanti anni ha la mamma/ il papà?
KWAHN-tee AHN-nee ah lah
MAHM-mah/ eel pah-PAH?

How old is mommy/ daddy?

Quante dita vedi?
KWAHN-teh DEE-tah VEH-dee?

How many fingers do you see?

Ce n'è una.
Cheh neh OO-nah.

There is only one.

Ci sono solamente quattro.
Chee SOH-noh soh-lah-MEHN-teh KWAHT-troh.

There are only four.

Io non ne ho.
EE-oh nohn neh oh.

I have none (of them).

Non ce ne sono.
Nohn cheh neh SOH-noh.

There are none.

Metti ognuno nel giusto posto.
MEHT-tee oh-NYOO-noh nehl
JYOOS-toh POHS-toh.

Put each one in the right place.

Quante ce ne sono?
KWAHN-teh cheh neh SOH-noh?

How many are there?

Tutti i biscotti sono stati mangiati.
TOOT-tee ee bees-KOHT-tee SOH-
noh STAH-tee mahn-JYAH-tee.

All the cookies have been
eaten.

Dopo quindici viene sedici.
DOH-poh KWEEN-dee-chee vee-
EH-neh SEH-dee-chee.

After 15 comes 16.

Conta da tre a dieci.
KOHN-tah dah treh ah dee-EH-chee.

Count from 3 to 10

Uno e uno sono due.
OO-noh eh OO-noh SOH-noh DOO-eh.

One and one make two.

Quattro meno tre fa uno.
KWAHT-troh MEH-noh treh fah
OO-noh.

Four minus three is one.

Due volte uno fa due.
DOO-eh VOHL-teh OO-noh fah
DOO-eh.

Two times one make two.

Sei diviso per due fa tre.
Say dee-VEE-zoh pehr DOO-eh fah treh.

Six divided by two make
three.

Due, quattro, sei sono numeri pari.
DOO-eh, KWAHT-troh, say
SOH-noh NOO-meh-ree PAH-ree.

Two, four, six are even
numbers.

Tre, cinque, sette sono numeri dispari.
Treh, CHEE-kway, SEHT-teh SOH-
noh NOO-meh-ree DEES-pah-ree.

Three, five, seven are odd
numbers.

Due metà
DOO-eh meh-TAH

Two halves

Una metà, un terzo, un quarto OO-nah meh-TAH, oon TEHR-tzoh, oon KWAHR-toh	One half, one third, one fourth
Un poco meno/ più Oon POH-koh MEH-noh/ pyoo	A little less/ more
Qualche/ alcuni KWAHL-keh/ ahl-KOO-nee	Some/ a few
Parecchi Pah-REHK-kee	Several
Molti MOHL-tee	Many, a lot

Numbers

zero DZEH-roh	0		sei say	6
uno OO-noh	1		sette SEHT-teh	7
due DOO-eh	2		otto OHT-toh	8
tre treh	3		nove NOH-veh	9
quattro KWAHT-troh	4		dieci dee-EH-chee	10
cinque CHEEN-kway	5			

Acorns   Buttons   Caterpillars

ALPHABET

a	b	c	d	e	f
ah	bee	chee	dee	eh	EHF-feh
g	h	i	k	l	m
gee	AHK-kah	ee	KAHP-pah	EHL-leh	EHM-meh
n	o	p	q	r	s
EH-neh	oh	pee	koo	EHR-reh	EHS-seh
t	u	v	w		x
tee	oo	voo	DOHP-pyah voo		eeks
y		z			
IHP-sil-ohn		ZEH-tah			

Che lettera è questa?
Keh LEHT-teh-rah eh KWEH-stah?

What letter is this?

Ecco la lettera A.
EHK-koh lah LEHT-teh-rah ah.

Here is the letter A.

Leggi questa lettera.
LEHJ-jee KWEHS-tah LEHT-teh-rah.

Read this letter.

Quante lettere ci sono nella parola
gatto?
KWAHN-teh LEHT-teh-reh chee
SOH-noh NEHL-lah pah-ROH-lah
GAHT-toh?

How many letters are
there in the word cat?

Dov'è la lettera H?
DOH-veh lah LEHT-teh-rah AHK-kah?

Where is the letter H?

Indica la lettera I.
Een-DEE-kah lah LEHT-teh-rah ee.

Point to the letter I.

Che cosa vuol dire questa parola?
Keh KOH-zah vwohl DEE-reh
KWEHS-tah pah-ROH-lah?

What does this word mean?

Di chi è questo nome?
Dee kee eh KWEHS-toh NOH-meh?

Whose name is this?

Non tenere la matita così stretta.
Nohn teh-NEH-reh lah mah-TEE-tah
koh-ZEE STREHT-tah.

Don't hold your pencil so
tight.

Tienila così.
TYEH-nee-lah koh-ZEE.

Hold it like this.

Per fare una L disegna una
linea in giù e una a destra.
Pehr FAH-reh OO-nah EHL-leh
dee-SEHN-yah OO-nah leen-EH-ah
een jyoo eh OO-nah ah DEHS-trah.

Write down and over for L.

PART 3

Vocabulary

Family and Other Persons

la mamma	mommy	il figlio	son
il papà	daddy	la sorella	sister
la nonna	grandmother	il fratello	brother
il nonno	grandfather	la donna	woman
la zia	aunt	l'uomo	man
lo zio	uncle	la ragazza	girl
la cugina	cousin (f)	il ragazzo	boy
il cugino	cousin (m)	i bambini	children
la nipote	niece	signorina	miss
il nipote	nephew	signora	missus
la nipote	granddaughter	signore	mister
il nipote	grandson		
la figlia	daughter		

Endearments

mia bambina (f)	my baby	mio bambino (m)	my baby
mia bambola	my doll	mio principe	my prince
mia principessa	my princess	caro/a	my dear
mio tesoro	my treasure		
	mio/a piccolo/a (m.f.)	my little one	

Colors

verde	green	blu	blue
nero/a	black	bianco/a	white
arancio/a	orange	rosso/a	red
giallo/a	yellow	violetto/a	violet
viola	violet	roso/a	pink
bruno/a	brown	grigio/a	grey
beige	beige		

Days of the Week

lunedì	Monday	martedì	Tuesday
mercoledì	Wednesday	giovedì	Thursday
venerdì	Friday	sabato	Saturday
domenica	Sunday		

Months of the Year

gennaio	January	febbraio	February
marzo	March	aprile	April
maggio	May	giugno	June
luglio	July	agosto	August
settembre	September	ottobre	October
novembre	November	dicembre	December

Seasons of the Year

la primavera	spring	l'autunno	autumn
l'estate	summer	l'inverno	winter

Holidays of the Year

compleanno	birthday	Festa del papà	Father's Day
Capodanno	New Year's Day		
compleanno di G. Washington	G. Washington's Birthday	Quattro di luglio	4th of July
compleanno di A. Lincoln	A. Lincoln's Birthday	Giorno della scoperta dell' America	Discovery of America
San Valentino	St. Valentine		
San Patrizio	St. Patrick	Festa d' Ognissanti	Halloween
La Pasqua	Easter		
La Pasqua Ebraica	Passover	Giorno del ringraziamento	Thanks- giving
Festa della mamma	Mother's Day	Natale	Christmas

Nursery

la vasca da bagno	bathtub	il libro	book
la carrozzina	carriage	il lettino	crib
il pannolino	diaper	il ciuccio	pacifier
il biberon	feeding bottle	il seggiolone	high chair
la sedia a dondola	rocking chair	il recinto	play pen
il passeggino	stroller	la spilla di sicurezza	safety pin
		il giocattolo	toy

Toys

l'aeroplano	airplane	la colla	paste
la palla	ball	il salva-danaio	piggy bank
il pallone	balloon	la marionetta	puppet
la mazza	bat	il puzzle	puzzle
la perlina	bead	il rastello	rake
la bicicletta	bicycle	il sonaglio	rattle
il cubo	block	l'anello	ring
la barca(a vela)	boat (sail)	il razzo	rocket
la livellatrice	bull dozer	il cavallo a dondolo	rocking horse
la corriera	bus	la corda	rope
l'automobile	car	la buca della sabbia	sand box
la scacchiera	chess board	le forbici	scissors
la creta	clay	il monopatino	scooter
il pagliaccio	clown	il dondolo	seesaw
il cowboy	cowboy	la vanga	shovel
il pastello	crayon	il pattino	skate
la bambola	doll	la slitta	sled
la casa delle bambole	doll house	lo scivolo	slide
il tamburo	drum	il soldatino (di piombo)	soldier (tin)
l'orechino	earring	(di legno)	(wood)
la canna da pesca	fishing rod	il sottomarino	submarine
la fortezza	fort	l'altalena	swing
il mappamondo	globe	il carro (armato)	tank (military)
l'elicottero	helicopter	il servizio da tè	tea set
il cerchio	hoop	l'orsacchiotto	Teddy bear
la tromba	horn	la racchetta	racquet
l'indiano/a	indian	la tenda	tent
la scatola a sorpresa	jack-in-the-box	la cima	top
la corda da saltare	jump-rope	la scatola dei giochi	toy box
l'aquilone	kite	il trattore	tractor
la biglia	marble	il treno (elettrico)	train (electric)
la maschera	mask	la triciclo	tricycle
la collana	necklace		
la scatola dei colori	paint box		
il pennello	paint brush		

Toys (cont)

il camion	truck	il carretto	wagon
(ribaltabile)	(dump)	la carriola	wheelbarrel
l'autocarro	truck	il fischietto	whistle
(rimorchio)	(tow)	lo xilofono	xylophone
(dei pompieri)	(fire)		
(dell'immondizia)	(garbage)		
(l'autobotte)	(oil)		

Clothing

l' accappatoio	bathrobe	la camicia	shirt
il costume di	bathing	la scarpa	shoe
bagno	suit	il lacio delle	shoe lace
la cintura	belt	scarpe	
il bavaglino	bib	le mutandine	shorts
la blusa	blouse	i pantaloni	slacks
lo stivale	boot	da donna	
il berretto	cap	la sottoveste	slip
il cappotto	coat	le pantofole	slippers
il vestito	dress	le scarpe da	sneakers
il guanto	glove	ginnastica	
il fazzoletto	handkerchief	la tuta da	snow suit
il cappello	hat	neve	
la giacca	jacket	la calza	sock
i jeans	jeans	la maglia	sweater
la camicia di	nightgown	la calzamaglia	tights
notte		l'ombrello	umbrella
la tuta	overalls	le mutandine	underpants
il soprabito	overcoat	la camiciola	undershirt
il pigiama	pajama	intima	
la borsa	pocketbook	la biancheria	underwear
l'impermeabile	raincoat	intima	
le calosce	rubbers	il portafoglio	wallet
i sandali	sandals		

Human Body

la caviglia	ankle	la mano	hand
il braccio	arm	la testa	head
la schiena	back	il talone	heel
il ventre	belly	il fianco	hip
l'ombellico	belly button	la mascella	jaw
la guancia	cheek	il ginocchio	knee
il petto	chest	la gamba	leg
la mente	chin	il labbro	lip
l'orecchio	ear	la bocca	mouth
il gomito	elbow	il collo	neck
l'occhio	eye	il naso	nose
il sopracciglio	eyebrow	la spalla	shoulder
la palpebra	eyelid	lo stomaco	stomach
gli occhi	eyes	la gola	throat
la faccia	face	il pollice	thumb
il dito	finger	il dito del	toe
l'unghia	finger nail	piede	
il piede	foot	la lingua	tongue
la fronte	forehead	il dente	tooth
i capelli	hair	la vita	waist
		il polso	wrist

Beverages

la birra	beer	il succo	orange
il cacao	cocoa	d'arancia	juice
il caffèlatte	coffee with milk	l'aranciata	orangeade
		la gazzosa	soda
la gazzosa (al limone)	lemon soda	una tazza di tè	a cup of tea
la limonata	lemonade	tè con limone	tea with lemon
il latte	milk		
il cioccolato (al latte)	milk (chocolate)	l'acqua (fredda)	water (iced)
		il vino	wine

Desserts

la torta di mele	apple pie	la frittella	fritter
		la gelatina	gelatin
il dolce	cake	il gelato	ice cream
lo zucchero	candy	la frittella	pancake
il biscotto	cookie	il budino	pudding
la crema	custard	il budino di riso	rice pudding
(caramella)	(caramel)		
(cioccolata)	(chocolate)		
(vanillia)	(vanilla)		

Vegetables

gli asparagi	asparagus	il prezzemolo	parsley
la barbabietola	beet	il pisello	pea
i cavolini	Brussel sprout	il pepe	pepper
il cavolfiore	cauliflower	la patata	potato
il sedano	celery	la zucca	pumpkin
il granturco	corn	il ravanello	radish
la pannocchia	(ear of) corn	gli spinaci	spinach
il cetriolo	cucumber	il fagiolino	stringbean
l 'aglio	garlic	il pomodoro	tomato
l'insalata	lettuce	la rapa	turnip
il fungo	mushroom		
la cipolla	onion		

Meats

la pancetta	bacon	la cotoletta	chop
la gallina	chicken	(di agnello)	(lamb)
(arrosto)	(roast)	(di maiale)	(pork)
il prosciutto	ham	la salsiccia	sausage
l'hamburger	hamburger	la bistecca	steak
		il tacchino	turkey

Fish

la carpa	carp	il gamberetto	shrimp
il merluzzo	cod	la sogliola	sole
l'aringa	herring	la trota	trout
l'aragosta	lobster	il tonno	tuna
il salmone	salmon		
la sardina	sardine		

Fruits

la mela	apple	il limone	lemon
la marmellata	apple	l'arancia	orange
di mele	sauce	la pesca	peach
la banana	banana	la pera	pear
la bacca	berry	l'ananas	pineapple
il mirtillo	blueberry	la susina	plum
la ciliegia	cherry	la prugna	prune
la noce di	coconut	secca	
cocco		l'uva passa	raisin
l'uva	grape	il lampone	raspberry
il pompelmo	grapefruit	la fragola	strawberry
		il mandarino	tangerine

Other Foods

il pane	bread	la frittella	pancake
il panino	bun, roll	l'arachide	peanut
il burro	butter	il burro di	peanut
il cereale	cereal	arachidi	butter
la gomma da	chewing	il pepe	pepper
masticare	gum	il sottoaceto	pickle
il cracker	cracker	i pop corn	pop corn
la panna	cream	la patatina	potato
la mollica	crumb	fritta	chip
l' uovo	egg	la zucca	pumpkin
(al tegamino)	(fried)	il riso	rice
(sodo)	(hard)	l'insalata	salad
(a la coque)	(soft)	il sale	salt
le patate fritte	French fries	i tramezzini	sandwich
il sugo	gravy	(di formaggio)	(cheese)
il miele	honey	la salsa	sauce
la marmellata	jam	i crauti	sauerkraut
la gelatina	jelly	la minestra	soup
il ketchup	ketchup	gli spaghetti	spaghetti
il pure di	mashed	lo stufato	stew
patate	potatoes	lo sciroppo	syrup
la cioccolata	milk	il toast	toast
	chocolate	l' aceto	vinegar

Tableware

la bottiglia	bottle	la pentola	pot
la ciotola	bowl	la casseruola	saucepan
la tazza	cup	il piattino	saucer
il piattino	dessert plate	la padella	skillet
la forchetta	fork	il piatto fondo	soup plate
il bicchiere	glass	la cucchiaio	spoon
il bollitore	kettle	lo zucchero	sugar
il coltello	knife	la tovaglia	tablecloth
il tovagliolo	napkin	il cucchiaio	tablespoon
la padella	pan	la teiera	teapot
la caraffa	pitcher	il cucchiaino	teaspoon
il piatto	plate	il vassoio	tray

Containers

il sacco	bag	la cassa	crate
la bottiglia	bottle	la busta	envelope
la scatola	box, can	il vasetto	jar
lo scatolone	carton	il coperchio	top, cover
		il tubo	tube

House

la soffitta	attic	il garage	garage
la porta servizio	back door	il cancello	gate
il cortile posteriore	back yard	il tubo	hose
la cantina	basement	la cucina	kitchen
il bagno	bathroom	l'annaffiatore da giardino	lawn sprinkler
la camera da letto	bedroom	il salotto	living room
la panchina	bench	la cassetta delle lettere	mailbox
il cespuglio	bush	il tetto	roof
il soffitto	ceiling	le scale	stairs
il comignolo	chimney	lo scalino	step
la camera da pranzo	dining room	la finestra	window
lo steccato	fence	il cortile	yard
l'aiuola	flower bed		

Dwellings

l'appartamento	appartment	l'albergo	hotel
la cabina	cabin	l'hotel	hotel
il condominio	condominium	la tenda	tent
la casetta	cottage	la roulotte	trailer
la casa di campagna	country house		

Kitchen

il grembiule	apron	il tavolo da stiro	ironing board
la ciotola	bowl	lo spazzolone	mop
la scopa	broom	il forno	oven
la vetrina	cabinet	il secchio	pail
l'orologio	clock	il lucido	polish
l'armadio	closet	la pentola	pot
l'asciugatrice	clothes dryer	il frigorifero	refriger- ator
la lavatrice	clothes washer	la macchina da cucire	sewing machine
il computer	computer	il lavello	sink
il banco	counter	la spazzola	scrub brush
il mobile	cupboard	la spugna	sponge
la scrivania	desk	lo sgabello	stool
il detersivo	detergent	la stufa	stove
lo strofinaccio	dish cloth	lo scolapasta	strainer
la lavastoviglie	dishwasher	il tavolo	table
il cassetto	drawer	il bollitore	tea kettle
il panno della polvere	dust cloth	il tostapane	toaster
il passo patate	electric beater	la macchina da scrivere	typewriter
l'imbuto	funnel	l'aspirapolvere	vacuum cleaner
la pattumiera	garbage pail		

Bedroom

il letto	bed	la fotografia	photograph
il copriletto	bedspread	il cuscino	pillow
la coperta	blanket	il manifesto	poster
il tappeto	carpet	la sedia a	rocking
l'armadio	closet	dondolo	chair
la tenda	curtain	lo scendiletto	rug (beside
la cassettiera	dresser		bed)
la lampada	lamp	il lenzuolo	sheet
lo specchio	mirror		

Living Room

il condiziona-	air condi-	il camino	fireplace
tore d'aria	tioner	il termosifone	heater
la poltrona	armchair	il pianoforte	piano
la libreria	bookcase	la radio	radio
lo scrittoio	desk	lo scaffale	shelf
		la televisione	television

Bathroom

l'aspirina	aspirin	la doccia	shower
la vasca	bath tub	il lavandino	sink
le bolle di	bubbles	il sapone	soap
sapone		la spugna	sponge
la crema per	face cream	il gabinetto	toilet
il viso		la carta	toilet
il rubinetto	faucet	igienica	paper
il rossetto	lipstick	lo spazzolino	tooth
lo smalto per	nail	da denti	brush
le unghie	polish	il dentifricio	toothpaste
il profumo	perfume		
la cipria	powder		

Entertainments

il luna park	amusement park	il parco	park
l'acquario	aquarium	il campo giochi	playground
il baseball	baseball	il ristorante	restaurant
la pallacanestro	basketball	il calcio	soccer
la spiaggia	beach	(fare)	(to go)
il campeggio	camping	acquisti	shopping
il circo	circus	il pattinaggio	skating
il concerto	concert	lo sci	skiing
andare a pesca	fishing	gli sport	sports
partita di calcio	football game	il nuoto	swimming
il gioco	game	una passeggiata	a walk
la ginnastica	gymnastics	lo zoo	zoo
escursione a piedi	hiking		
il cinema	movie theatre		
il museo	museum		
la festa	party		

Tools

il trapano	drill	la carta vetrata	sandpaper
il martello	hammer	la sega	saw
la zappa	hoe	le forbici	scissors
la scala a pioli	ladder	la vite	screw
la falciatrice	lawn mower	il giravite	screw-driver
il chiodo	nail	la vanga	shovel
il dado	nut	il trapiantatoio	trowel
il forcone	pitchfork	la morsa	vise
le pinze	pliers	la carriola	wheelbarrow
il rastrello	rake	la chiave inglese	wrench

Along the Road

l'aeroporto	airport	il parcheggio	parking lot
gli appartamenti	apartments		
il guasto	breakdown	la posta	post office
il ponte	bridge	i gabinetti	restrooms
l' edificio	building	la strada	road
l'autobus	bus	il marciapiede	sidewalk
la stazione degli autobus	bus station	il segnale	sign post
		il limite di velocita	speed limit
la fermata dell'autobus	bus stop	l'automobile sportiva	sports car
la macchina	car	la scuola	school
la chiesa	church	la strada	street
l'angolo	corner	il palo della luce	street light
le strisce	crossing		
il bordo	curb	il supermercato	supermarket
la fabbrica	factory		
la fattoria	farm	il taxi	taxi
il campo	field	una cabina telefonica	telephone booth
la caserma dei pompieri	fire house		
l'autopompa	fire truck	il palo telefonico	telephone pole
la stazione di servizio	gas station	i binari	tracks
		il traffico	traffic
la pompa della benzina	gas pump	la rotatoria	traffic circle
la siepe	hedge		
l' autostrada	highway	l'ingorgo del traffico	traffic jam
la buca	hole	il semaforo	traffic light
l'ospedale	hospital		
la casa	house	il treno	train
una buca delle lettere	mail box	la stazione	train station
la motocicletta	motorcycle	il carro (attrezzi)	truck (tow)
parcheggiare	to park	il camion	truck
		il tunnel	tunnel
		il furgone	van

The Car

la batteria	battery	il sedile	seat
lo sportello	door	lo sterzo	steering wheel
le luci	headlights		
il clacson	horn	il copertone	tire
il motore	motor	la ruota	wheel

Stores

il panificio	bakery	la farmacia	drug store
la banca	bank	il negoziante di mobili	furniture store
il salone	barber shop		
il instituto di bellezza	beauty shop	gli alimentari	grocers
		il negoziante di gioielli	jewelry store
la macelleria	butcher shop		
la lavanderia a secco	cleaners	la lavanderia automatica	laundromat
il negoziante di vestiti	clothing store	il deposito di legname	lumber yard
la latteria	dairy store	il vivaio	nursery
il grande magazzino	department store	il magazzino di scarpe	shoe store

Occupations

l'attore	actor	il negoziante	merchant
l'astronauta	astronaut	il sacerdote	minister
il panettiere	baker	l'indossatore	model (m)
il macellaio	butcher	l'indossatrice	model (f)
il carpentiere	carpenter	l'infermiera	nurse (f)
l'autista	chauffeur	l'imbianchino	painter
il cuoco	chef	farmacista	pharmacist
il cowboy	cowboy	il pilota	pilot
il dentista	dentist	il poliziotto	policeman
il dottore	doctor	il sacerdote	priest
l' ingegnere	engineer	il pilota	race car driver
il contadino	farmer		
il pompiere	fireman	il marinaio	sailor
il pescatore	fisherman	il commesso	salesman
il meccanico	garage mechanic	la commessa	saleswoman
il netturbino	garbage man	il tassista	taxidriver
il giardiniere	gardener	il macchinista	train engineer
il parrucchiere	hair dresser		
l'avvocato	lawyer	la cameriera	waitress
il bibliotecario	librarian (m)	il cameriere	waiter
la bibliotecaria	librarian (f)	il guardiano dello zoo	zoo keeper
il postino	mailman		

Animals

l'orso	bear	il lama	llama
il toro	bull	la talpa	mole
il cammello	camel	la scimmia	monkey
il gatto	cat	il topo	mouse
la mucca	cow	il bue	ox
il coccodrillo	crocodile	il panda	panda
il cervo	deer	il maiole	pig
il cane	dog	il porcellino	piglet
l'asino	donkey	il pony	pony
l'elefante	elephant	il cucciolo	puppy
il cerbiatto	fawn	il coniglio	rabbit
la volpe	fox	il procione	raccoon
la rana	frog	il ratto	rat
la giraffa	giraffe	la renna	reindeer
la capra	goat	il gallo	rooster
il gorilla	gorilla	la foca	seal
la cavia	guinea pig	la pecora	sheep
il criceto	hamster	il serpente	snake
l'ippopotamo	hippopotamus	lo scoiattolo	squirrel
il cavallo	horse	la tigre	tiger
il canguro	kangaroo	la tartaruga	turtle
il gattino	kitten	la balena	whale
l'agnello	lamb	il lupo	wolf
il leopardo	leopard	il lombrico	worm (earth)
il leone	lion	la zebra	zebra

Birds

il canarino	canary	il gufo	owl
il pulcino	chick	il pellicano	pelican
il pollo	chicken	il piccione	pigeon
l' anatra	duck	il pettirosso	robin
l' anatroccolo	duckling	il gabbiano	seagull
l'oca	goose	il passero	sparrow
il papero	gosling	il cigno	swan
		il tacchino	turkey

Insects

la formica	ant	la cavalletta	grasshopper
l'ape	bee	la coccinella	lady bug
la farfalla	butterfly	la zanzara	mosquito
il bruco	caterpillar	il lepidottero	moth
la blatta	cockroach	la mantide	praying
il grillo	cricket	religiosa	mantis
la pulce	flea	il ragno	spider
la mosca	fly	la vespa	wasp

Trees

il melo	apple	il pero	pear
il ciliegio	cherry	il pino	pine
l'acero	maple	l' abete	spruce
la quercia	oak	il salice	willow

Flowers

l'azalea	azalea	il lilla	lilac
il ranuncolo	buttercup	il mughetto	lily of the
il garofano	carnation		valley
il crisantemo	chrysanthemum	la mimosa	mimosa
il croco	crocus	l'orchidea	orchid
il giglio	daffodil	la pensée	pansy
la dalia	dahlia	la peonia	peony
il dente di	dandelion	la petunia	petunia
leone		il rododendro	rhododendron
la gardenia	gardenia	la rosa	rose
il geranio	geranium	il tulipano	tulip
l'iris	iris	la viola	violet

READING GUIDANCE

ABC's of SAT's: How One Student Scored 800 on the Verbal SAT
c. 2000 Illustrated; 146 pp   ISBN#: 0-9606140-9-5
Ages: *Birth to 12 years*   Grades: Pre-school to middle school $18.95

An *annotated* list of hundreds of books starting with pre-natal readings and concluding with titles for 13-year olds. This is not only the collective readings of a *Merit Scholar* who aced the verbal SAT with a perfect score of 800, but a list of books children will love and enjoy for their own merit. A list of exciting, enjoyable books, and a pain-free preparation for test-taking! A perfect combination.

INDEX

to fall	cadire 68,94,111	fruit	la frutta 101
fast	veloce 87,106	full	piena 50,109
father	papà 82	funny	comico/a 70
faucet	il rubinetto 41		
fault	la colpa 68		
to feed	dar da mangiare 22, 50,91	G	
to fight	fare a pugni 29	game	il gioco 79
to fill	riempire 51	garage	l'autorimessa 84
finger	il dito 33,56,114	garbage	il secchio dell'
fingernail	l'unghia 41,45	bag	immondizia 61
to finish	finire 51	garden	il giardino 61
Fire!	Fuoco! 91	gasoline	la benzina 84
first	primo 19	gas station	il distributore di
fish	il pesce 50		benzina 63
to fit	adattare 95	gently	dolcemente 22
to float	galleggiare 103	gently	piano 91,94
floor	il pavimento 58,91	gently	con dolcezza 35
flour	la farina 59	to get	prendere18
flower	il fiore 85	(capture)	
to fly	volare 104	to get up	alzarsi 44
fog	la nebbia 110	giraffe	la giraffa 23
to fold	piegare 43,60,90	to give	dare 22,28
to follow	seguire 38	to give up	smettere 78
food	il cibo 49	glad	contento/a 68
foot	il piede 17,20,31, 86,95	gland	la ghiandola 56
		glass	il bicchiere 51
to forget	dimenticare 31,37, 40	glasses	gli occhiali 104
		glove	il guanto 45
fork	la forchetta 49	to go	andare 16,21,31,
form	la forma 107		32,34,38
(in) four	in quattro 90	to go	funzionare 84
free	libero/a 81	(engine)	
friend	l'amico 81	to go out	uscire 38
to frighten	fare paura 11	to go out	andare fuori 84
(in)front of	davanti 93	to go to sleep	dormire 54

goal	il gol 96	head	la testa 12
God	Dio 54	to hear	sentire 11
goodbye	arrivederci 18	heavy	pesante 53
to grab	prendere 33	Help!	Aiuto! 68,91
gray	grigio/a 110	to help	aiutare 46,57,59
green	verde 32	to help	prendere 48
grocer's	la drogheria 64	oneself	
ground	la terra 33	here	qui 18
to grow	crescere 61	Here is	Ecco 13,15,17
to growl	ringhiare 83	to hide	nascondere 92
		high	forte 93
		hill	la collina 106
	H	to hit	dare pugni 27
		to hit	colpire 86
hair	i capelli 46	to hold	tenere 12,14,94,
half-way	a metà 20		95,99
hammer	il martello 62	to hold	agguantare 86
to hammer	piantare 62	to hold	prendere 33
hand	la mano 17,20,28,33	hoop	il cerchio 93,,98
handkerchief	il fazzoletto 97	to hop	saltellare 83
handlebar	il manubrio 86	to hope	sperare 70
handsome	bello 76	hopscotch	campana 82
to hang	appendere 43,53	horse	il cavallo 11
hanger	la stanpella 53	hot	caldo/a 42
to happen	succedere 35,71	to hug	abbracciare 74
happy	contento/a 23	hump	la gobba 83
hard	duro/a 106	hungry	avere fame 107
hardware	la feramenta 63	in a hurry	avere fretta 28
store		Hurry!	Muoviti! 31
hat	il cappello 45,79	to hurry	sbrigarci 31
to have	avere 21	to hurt	fare male 16,36
to have a	divertire 104	to hurt	farsi male 87
good time		oneself	
to have just	avere appena 102		

I

ice cream	il gelato 79
immediately	immediata-mente 38
inside	dentro 84
interesting	interessante 70
to invite	invitare 79
to iron	stirare 60

J

jacket	la giacca 45
juice	il succo 51
juicy	al sangue 50
to jump	saltare 31,85,93,94

K

kangaroo	il canguro 83
to keep	tenere 86
to kick	dare calci 15,27
kiss	il bacio 54,74
kitchen	la cucina 31,81
kite	l'aquilone 94
knee	il ginocchio 42
knife	il coltello 33,49
to knock down	gettare 97
to know	sapere 80

L

to land	atterrare 82,104
language	la lingua 35
lap	la ginocchia 12
large	grande 13,67
later	tardi 28
laundromat	la lavanderia 64
laundry	la biancheria 60
lawn	l'erba del prato 61
to lay down	mettere 91
leader	il capo 92
leaf	la foglia 61
to leak	perdere 94
to lean out	sporgersi 30
to leave	partire 107
to leave, let	lasciare 30,35,85
leg	la gamba 89
Let go!	Molla! 12
letter	la lettera 117
library	la biblioteca 117
to lie down	sdraiarsi 35
life-guard	il bagnino 102
to lift	alzare 95
light	la luce 32,39,43,54
lightening	la fulmina 110
to like	piacere 13,18,43, 50,77,78
line	la lenza 92
to listen	ascoltare 35
a little	un poco 49
to load up	caricare 97

P

R

rain	la pioggia 109,110,
to rain	piovere 109
rainbow	l'arcobaleno 110
to rake	rastrellare 61
rattle	il sonaglio 12,15,97
to read	leggere 52,60,117
ready	pronto/a/ 47,53
red	rosso/a 45
refreshing	rinfrescante 102
refrigerator	il frigorifero 30
to remember	recordare 37
to rent	noleggiare 105
to rest	riposare 107
restaurant	il ristorante 79
to return	rendere 65
to ring	sonare 17,87
rink	la pista di
	pattinaggio 95
ripe	maturo/a 49
rock, stone	il sasso 34
to rock	dondolare 35
to roll	arrotolare 90
to roll	rotolare 98
room	la camera 34,60
rooster	il gallo 83
rope	la corda 94
rough	mosso/a 101
row	la fila 61
to rub	strofinare 36
rug	il tapeto 31,58
to run	correre 31,89
to run	preparare 42
(a bath)	
runway	la pista
	d'atteraggio 83

S

sad	triste 23,68
to sail	fare vela 89
sale	la svendita 65
salesman	il commesso 66
saleswoman	la commessa 66
salt	il sale 49
salty	salato/a 50
sand	la sabbia 97,103
to sand	strofinare con la
	carta vetrata 62
sandbox	la cassa di
	sabbia 84
sandwich	il panino 48,101
sauce	il sugo 50
to saw	segare 62
to say	dire 11,33
to score	fare un
(goal)	gol 96
to scratch	graffiare 55
screwdriver	il cacciavite 62
sea	il mare 101
sea shell	la conchiglia 102
seat	la sedia 22
seaweed	l'alga 103
to see	vedere 14,34,66,89,98
seed	il seme 61
to send	chiamare 91
for help	
to set(table)	apparecchiare 57
shade	l'ombra 101
to shake	scuotere 97
sharp	affilato/a 33
to sharpen	affilare 95
shirt	la camicia 34,44,53

Also by Therese Slevin Pirz

Speak French to Your Baby
Speak Spanish to Your Baby

For a successful foreign language program speak to your children in the foreign language everyday using —

Kids Stuff Series:	**Language Helper Series:**
Kids Stuff Spanish	Language Helper Spanish
Kids Stuff French	
Kids Stuff German	Language Helper German
Kids Stuff Italian	
Kids Stuff Russian	Language Helper Russian
Kids Stuff Chinese	
Kids Stuff Inglés	Language Helper Inglés
Kids Stuff Angliiski (English)	Language Helper Angliiski (English)
Kids Stuff Yingyu (English) (2008)	

ABCs of SATs: How One Student Scored 800 on the Verbal SAT
(Reading Guidance for children 1 month to 13 years)